Following The Yellow Brick Road

The Adult Child's Personal Journey Through Oz

Joy Erlichman Miller
Marianne Leighton Ripper

Illustrated by Diana Burlison

Health Communications, Inc.
Deerfield Beach, Florida

Marianne Ripper
Joy Miller
Co-Directors
Family Interventions
4700 North Prospect Road
Peoria Heights, Illinois 61614

*Special thanks to Turner Entertainment for permission
to utilize the analogy of "The Wizard of Oz."*

©*1939 Loew's Incorporated
Ren. 1966 Metro-Goldwyn-Mayer, Inc.*

Library of Congress Cataloging-in-Publication Data
Miller, Joy, 1950-
  Following the yellow brick road.

  Bibliography: p.
  1. Co-dependence (Psychology) 2. Children of
alcoholic parents — Mental health. 3. Baum, L. Frank
(Lyman Frank), 1856-1919. Wizard of Oz. I. Ripper,
Marianne, 1952-   II. Title.
RC569.5.C63M54   1987   616.89   87-26431
ISBN 0-932194-61-3

Published by: Health Communications, Inc.
        Enterprise Center
        3201 S.W. 15th Street
        Deerfield Beach, FL 33442

Acknowledgments

The *Glenda* in my life has been **Marianne Ripper**. She has given me the greatest gift that anyone could give to another — a belief in myself. She allowed me to be creative, to explore the possibilities and discover what was hiding deep within. She has been my support, my caring, my confidant, and my teacher along my journey. Her gift was allowing me to find me, and most importantly, the gift of sharing herself. No words can fully explain my gratitude and love. You surely have made my journey "joyous".

— *Joy*

This acknowledgment is written with love and respect to my *Glenda*. **Joy Miller** has been more than just a partner; she has also become an intimate friend. Without Joy's constant prodding of me, this book would never have been possible. She gave me not only encouragement, honesty and constructive criticism, but most of all, her love and friendship. Together we went over the rainbow and made our dreams come true.

— *Marianne*

Munchkins: Our journey would not have been possible if not for those who have shared their struggles, their joys, and their journeys. Our journey has been enriched because you dared to find yourselves. You have found the answers within yourselves and now have come home! Our love, gratitude and thanks to **Cindy, Laura, Ann, Dot, Gladys, Rose, Rick, Bill, Barb, Pat, Diane, Jan, Sandy, Gary, Amy and Sue.**

Lollipop Guild: **Dot and Jean** — You have successfully helped us enter the Emerald City. Your constant, vigilant editing has helped us realize our dreams. **Diana** — your illustrations have made our journey very special — just as you are special. Your gift is the beauty of an artist. Our thanks!

Residents of Emerald City: There have been so many that have been there to help us along our journey. Your support and love have given us the courage to go forward. Our special thanks to all of our clients and friends who have supported our journey into Oz.

Ballerina: **Jodi** — You gracefully danced through all the mayhem. You never batted an eye. You were our support and our strength. Without you, we surely would have fallen asleep in the "Poppy Fields". You have given us a special friendship on our journey to Oz.

Doorman of the Castle in the Emerald City: You held the key and allowed us to enter. You believed in us so we could find our strength within. Your encouragement kept us moving onward. Our love and thanks to **Gary, Peter** and **Marie** at Health Communications. A special thanks to **Debbie** who unconditionally believed in us and *saw* in us what others could not see . . . we love you!

Professor Marvel: To all of the pioneers in the Children of Alcoholics movement. You have been our mentors — thank you for your courage, sensitivity, and your knowledge. Because of you, we could feel confident to journey forward. A special thanks to **Rokelle Lerner:** You are a special loving friend whose sensitivity and playfulness is something we respect and admire — you helped us believe in ourselves!

Auntie Em and Uncle Henry: Our families: **Mom** and **Dad** — you gave me a "namesake" — but more importantly, you gave me something to believe in — myself. You taught me how to love and how to care! You have given my life a special glowing force that will live within me forever. My deepest love and thanks!

— *Joy*

Mom and Dad: You gave me the unquestioning direction in the quest for knowledge. You taught me that the family can be delicate and must be nurtured with love. Because of the morals and values you instilled in me I have been able to have the family of my dreams.

— *Marianne*

Toto: They say that a dog is a man's best friend — but, **John**, you have always been my best friend, my husband, my lover and my support. You have always been there, urging me to chase my dreams, always there telling me to go forward. You are a gift from God, my endless love! — *Joy*

Dorothy had Toto by her side for love, support and to ease her fears. My Toto is my husband **John**, who has never doubted my abilities and not only supported but also encouraged every risk I have undertaken. You have given me freedom to grow and enabled our special love to prosper and grow. We have an unconditional love that will last us a lifetime. — *Marianne*

Mayor: My son **Josh** — You are beginning your journey. Listen to your heart and your brain, and be fearless in your dreams. You hold the Ruby Slippers — you can be anything that you desire as long as you believe in yourself! I love you! — *Joy*

Jessica, you possess the curiosity of the Munchkins which will allow you to continue to question, take risks and grow. Your heart is as big as the Tin Man's, your brain just beginning to expand and your courage is as large as the roar of the Lion. Although it is inevitable that you will trip and fall, your courage, knowledge and heart will give you the strength to pick yourself up and move in any direction you choose. — *Marianne*

Contents

Foreword

This is not a fairy tale. *Following The Yellow Brick Road: The Adult Child's Personal Journey Through Oz* is written for Adult Children of Alcoholics and other children of trauma. We believe that the story of Dorothy in the *Wizard of Oz* is an excellent analogy to illustrate how Adult Children of Alcoholics have used unhealthy survival techniques as a means of dealing with life.

Dorothy's journey home illustrates her personal path to finding the strength within herself. We believe that your personal journey with us into the Land of Oz will have you saying, "There's no place like home!"

1

Journey Into Oz

Dorothy Gale opens her eyes with fear. She realizes she has lived through the trauma of the tornado. Only moments ago she recalls the horror of feeling abandoned by Auntie Em and Uncle Henry. She feels the shame and guilt for leaving her family. Perhaps she deserved them leaving her alone in the storm. "Where were they?" The shock of total aloneness is comforted by Toto as they run into the home that was "supposed to be" a place of safety.

After the storm, scared and terrified, Dorothy inches toward the door of the Kansas farm house. Cautiously, she opens the door that transforms her "black and white" world into a place of splendor. Dorothy gazes mystified at the colorful beauty and tranquility, unable to move. She looks around and states, "I have a feeling we aren't in Kansas anymore . . . we must be over the rainbow." As Dorothy stares spellbound at the brilliant colors, a bubble floats down holding Glenda, the Good Witch of the North. Glenda, the Good Witch, is always there to guide Dorothy through her perilous travels.

But, it is Dorothy who finds *within herself* the key to happiness.

This story typifies the recovery process of an Adult Child of an Alcoholic in treatment. Just as Dorothy was terrified by the impending tornado, children in an alcoholic world also feel the terror. They too experience shame, guilt, fear and terror as Dorothy did that autumn day in Kansas. But for the child who grows up in an alcoholic home, every day is like having a tornado pass through the house. Will the house survive? Will I be ripped to shreds? Every day is filled with the possibility of terror.

Just as Dorothy was amazed by the beauty and splendor of Oz, so too is the recovering Adult Child amazed by the rewards of therapy. Recovering Adult Children remark that their worlds are not the same. It's not Kansas at all — life in recovery is like being over the rainbow. The world that was black and white for the Adult Child becomes one of color and emanates a feeling of being truly alive. Each step into Oz is an unknown risk for the Adult Child.

Just as Glenda guided Dorothy through her journey, we hope to guide you through *your* recovery. We hope to give you some clues to finding your way back home. We are confident we can also alert you to impending pitfalls — the bad witches in your progress.

Dorothy had the power *within herself* to risk the journey home but she needed Glenda's guidance to discover the abilities within herself. We can only guide your trip. You must take the first step. Join us in the colorful journey into recovery — the Land of Oz.

2

Leaving the Black and White World Behind

(The Six Steps Used By ACoAs)

You have dared to leave the black and white world of Kansas to join us in a glorious journey into the technicolor visualization of Oz. Leaving the black and white world of Kansas is quite scary — we truly understand. You have no concept of what you will encounter in Oz as we journey through this book together. The risk will be worthwhile — you will find the beauty within your grasp . . .

Dorothy slowly opens the door of her black and white farmhouse. As she peers cautiously through the doorway, she is amazed by the blaze of color that greets her. She leaves her black and white world behind upon entering Munchkin Country, a place filled with magnificent daisies, buttercups and poppies. Flowers grow everywhere to amazing proportions and vibrant splendor. Dorothy is totally caught up in the beauty of the land "over the rainbow".

J

As you may recall, Dorothy's life in Kansas was filmed in black and white. It wasn't until she went over the rainbow that color became a part of her world. This depicts the life of an Adult Child of an Alcoholic. We live in a world that teaches us how to survive, but not how to *enjoy* life. A black and white world consists of extremes. Things are wonderful or a catastrophe, right or wrong, good or bad, positive or negative. Life is like living on an unpredictable roller coaster — up one minute, down the next and we never know when the bottom will fall out.

While Dorothy was in Kansas, she could only dream of a place "somewhere over the rainbow". It was not until the tornado hit that she was forced to find the place of which she had only dreamt. Change is something we usually avoid unless we have a crisis which forces us to do something different. Dorothy's crisis was the tornado.

One of the best analogies of traveling from the world of black and white into the land of Oz is going through the stages of grief as Elisabeth Kubler-Ross describes them. These stages, from *"On Death and Dying"* will aid our journey into recovery:

1. I'm totally alone (Isolation)
2. Running away is the answer (Denial)
3. I'm afraid to show you how mad I am (Anger)
4. I'll go home if everything is okay (Bargaining)
5. The hopelessness of the Scarecrow (Depression)
6. We're not in Kansas anymore (Acceptance)

Remember as you read through each stage that the statements and the behaviors associated with that stage were learned as a means of survival in your family of origin. These behaviors have continued into our adult lives. It is important to realize that both positive and negative behaviors were learned through our experiences.

Initially, we are convinced by our families that our

way of reacting to situations is the only way. We use these skills in our adult lives, not realizing that the world we grew up in is different than the world we are attempting to live in now. Situations that are common, everyday occurrences in one household may not be common in a dysfunctional household.

For example, an ACoA Catholic priest named John stated that the first time he experienced differences between his family and other families was when he stayed overnight at a friend's house. His friend's father didn't vomit upon arising in the morning. John remarked that his first thought was, "There must be something wrong with my friend's father." John assumed that his friend's father was abnormal because John's father got sick every morning. It wasn't until years later John realized it was *his* father who was abnormal. When a revelation such as this is made and clarity of thinking occurs, it's like Dorothy realizing she is not in Kansas anymore — a breakthrough in denial!

Your journey through some steps may take weeks, while other parts of your journey may take years. Remember as you travel through Oz that it is *a journey, not a destination!*

Please note that your journey will evoke some feelings about your family of origin. The tendency is to blame our parents for the lives we had as children and subsequently our lives as adults. As we break through the denial and change the patterns of our lives, we come to learn the following: (1) our parents did the best parenting they knew; (2) our parents parented through their own experiences from their parents (as we are parenting or would parent without changes); (3) our parents did not set out to hurt us intentionally; and (4) we cannot continue to blame our parents for what we continue to do. Instead we need to take responsibility for ourselves.

Are you ready to take Step One?

| 0 |

Step 1: Totally Alone (Isolation)

The dastardly old Miss Gulch demands that Toto be taken from the tearful Dorothy. Expecting protection from Uncle Henry, Dorothy sobs for a saviour for her beloved dog. Uncle Henry reluctantly puts Toto in Miss Gulch's basket prison. Dorothy's precious Toto is taken from her as she retreats to her bedroom in utter despair. Toto becomes the prisoner of Miss Gulch as Dorothy tearfully mourns her loss in her room — isolated and alone!

The first step in the acceptance of being an ACoA is recognition of the isolation. As ACoAs, we have learned from birth that we can't count on family, especially our mother and father, to be there for us emotionally. For some of us, not only have we learned that parents will not be there emotionally, but they will also not be there physically. We have taught ourselves to be self-dependent for anything and everything. This self-taught independence rejects anyone who wants to get close emotionally or physically. The self-taught response is, "If my parents can't love me, then I must be unlovable," or "If I can't trust Mom or Dad to be there emotionally, how can I possibly trust anyone else to be there for me?" (most likely an unconscious statement).

The denial pattern that accompanies isolation is a pattern of avoidance. We grow up being taught to keep the family secret(s): alcoholism, incest, verbal abuse or other problems that caused the dysfunction within the family. We were actually taught not to see things as they really are and to avoid the problems. This avoidance technique allowed the family a denial system by which *no one* had to deal with the problem. By avoiding reality we are forced to use unhealthy survival skills which become avoidance patterns. These patterns are reinforced by use of repetition. The following avoidance patterns are common:

A. KEEP AWAY BY DEFAULT

ACoAs are skilled at choosing people who will allow us to deny the reality of the family secrets. In fact, we not only choose people to help deny, but also choose people who will help us continue utilizing our unhealthy survival skills. We unconsciously set up situations which keep others distanced while keeping us in the middle of all the uproar. Perhaps some of these statements sound familiar: "I've got to get this family together", "I don't have time for trivial matters, I've got real problems in the family that I have to solve", "Who has time for fun?", "I can't slow down and think about myself or something terrible will happen", "This family can't function without me", or "It's not me with the problems, it's . . .".

Other default skills include the use of rationalization when the feelings of fear emerge. The rationale is: "If I just ignore it, I'm sure it will go away" or "If I accomplish enough, I'll be okay, and everything will turn out all right."

Another clever unconscious manipulation is an attempt to stay away from the issues by shifting attention to others. The distorted survival thinking incorporates the concept of diverting attention so that hopefully the problem will go away.

B. KEEP AWAY BY DISTRACTION

A common technique which encourages isolation is the practice of distracting others. The rationale is, "If I create enough crises, I can feel worthwhile by being able to fix the crises and the people in the crises. Additionally, if I can have people look at the mess and then see what I accomplished, I must be worthwhile."

A young client named Karen had associated pain with love as a result of seeing her parents constantly fighting during her childhood. Whenever she questioned her mother as to why she remained in the marriage, her mother replied, "I love him". At that time, the message implanted was that "pain equals love". With this mixed message Karen continued the pattern in her own marriage by creating crisis after crisis, thinking she was proving her love to her husband.

There are two means of distraction.

1. Overwhelm by Flooding

With this method we discover all the effects, problems and textbook solutions for the family in crisis. Unfortunately, we are flooded with information but we do not relate it to our own lives. This denial process can be illustrated by the following:

Mike, who is an alcoholic, has been in therapy intermittently over the past nine years. Only recently Mike realized that his inability to maintain any lasting sobriety was a result of his highly dysfunctional alcoholic family of origin. Beginning to address his ACoA issues, he requested his sister join him in his therapy sessions.

His sister Carol was able to explain the family's behaviors in detail, using professional terminology. When questioned about the terminology, she reported that she was a psychology major. She continued by explaining that the dysfunctional family behaviors only affected Mike and the rest of the family. They had no real effect on her. She added, "Besides, I know too much to let this affect me." Unfortunately, Carol learned all about her father's and Mike's alcoholism and abusive behavior in order to deny the impact they had made on her. She had become aware of the dysfunction in the family but had not integrated the awareness into her

U

own life. She had used **selective denial.** This selective denial promoted her movement into the role of Family Enabler (caretaker) after her mother's death. Ironically, it was later discovered that Carol's resentments and anger centered around her mother's role as that of the family Enabler.

2. The Roar of the Lion

The "roar" is a means of distraction used to keep everything in a mess so that we can run in and fix it or make the situation better. We set out to systematically create real crises while giving the constant message, "You cannot survive without me." The real paradox is that we can't survive without the crises. The need for crises and excitement is not on a conscious level but on an unconscious level as a means of survival, as well as a means of attempting to gain a positive self-worth.

A real crisis can occur when there is no one within the family to blame. This is commonly experienced when a significant person, who is a Scapegoat, stops being the family's scapegoat. For example, Wendy was not only an ACoA, but she was also married to an active alcoholic. She, of course, entered therapy because of her husband's alcoholism. Her one wish was that her husband would gain and maintain sobriety. She decided to orchestrate a professional intervention for her husband and as a result, her husband went into treatment at a nearby hospital.

After Wendy's husband had successfully completed inpatient treatment and was in sobriety for over two months, Wendy reported that she couldn't stand her husband's behavioral changes. Wendy felt as though she had lost all of her control over the family. She complained that her husband now wanted to discipline the children and know where the money was being spent. In discussing her situation, Wendy realized that not only was her husband wanting to take over *his* responsibilities around the house and with the family, but he was now taking responsibility for *himself*. This left her without an external focus or scapegoat. She was then able to see that she was frightened at the thought of being forced to take responsibility only for herself. Wendy stated, "Now, if I make a mistake, I don't have anyone to blame." With terror in her eyes she said, "What if he gets healthy and doesn't want me anymore?"

Wendy needed to learn that she was allowed to make mistakes and that her husband could love her for being Wendy, not for what she did for him. She also had to learn how to be involved in an intimate relationship with her husband. Wendy addressed her compulsive dependency on her husband and then began clarifying personal boundaries for her own recovery program.

Step 2: Running Away (Denial)

Toto is able to cleverly escape the terrifying clutches of Miss Gulch and immediately scrambles home to the safety of Dorothy's arms. Dorothy realizes that this means imminent danger for the escapee, and she knows the only answer is to run away from home. As Toto yips, she quickly covers the escapee with a blanket as they run down the dusty road, leaving the farmhouse behind. Dorothy truly believes she can leave all her problems behind as she nears the wagon of Professor Marvel. Running away is the only answer.

The second stage is denial. Denial increases the intensity of the crisis. Ironically, what we do is create more and more crises in an attempt to regain control. This only increases the feelings of being overwhelmed and increases our feelings of being out of control. This pattern continues until we feel like we are going crazy. Because of our need to control, as well as our fear of depending on someone, we hold the fear, uncertainty, low self-worth and devastation a secret.

Martha, an ACoA, is married to a "dry" alcoholic. Because he was "dry", and not recovering, he simply continued his manipulations without the aid of the alcohol. Martha was the Responsible Child in her family of origin and was always called upon when the family was in a crisis (which was at least bi-monthly). In talking with Martha about her family of origin, she said, "I have to deny that my family is crazy because if I admit *they* have problems, then *I* must have problems. I am such a pillar of strength in my family that if they think something is wrong with me, they couldn't exist!"

During one session Martha realized that she couldn't control *others* but that she could take control over what *she* does. Martha responded by saying, "But if I don't attempt to control them, they will drive me crazy!" As the session continued, Martha described her feelings of going crazy and her desperate need to learn how to control her husband, son and family of origin. In processing her methods of attempting to gain control of others and the results that followed, she admitted, "The thing that I thought was going to save me (having control of others) is actually what is destroying me."

As a result of attempting to control others, she actually gave up her own control and was herself manipulated and controlled. The result for Martha was that she was having feelings of depression and thoughts of going crazy. Another way of running away is by physical means. We think that if we move far enough away from our family of origin, we will rid ourselves of the problems.

When going through the Running Away (Denial) stage, either physically or mentally, we may question our role in the problems but quickly dismiss having any involvement by convincing ourselves that, "It's not me, it's my husband." There are many variations of the "It's

R

not me, it's . . ." self-statement. The following are three examples of such denial self-statements:

A. ABSOLUTELY NOT

While in "absolutely not", we make statements like: "I'm not the one with the problems, I'm the one who is fixing the problems", or "The only reason I feel this way is because of the problems everyone else is throwing at me." We *systematically deny* the reality of the effects. We may even *absolutely deny* the problem of alcoholism in the family by minimizing. In Martha's case she dismissed the manipulations of her husband, as well as the continued effects of alcoholism on her life, because her husband was not actually drinking. She believed that the only thing wrong in her marriage was alcohol.

B. REASONING THE TRUTH AWAY

This distorted thinking process keeps our fantasy world alive and active. Many of us who take the Responsible role will make our first contact with a psychotherapist for a dual purpose: (1) to help someone else who is in pain and (2) to gather information to use as proof that *we* are all right. We become experts on the facts concerning the disease of alcoholism but never apply the information to ourselves. We focus on those facts learned in therapy that will help prove to others that we could not *possibly* have any problems. We talk so clearly, confidently, rationally and responsibly that others not only question what they have been experiencing, but come to believe that we must know exactly what we are talking about. This is a powerful usage of intellectualization which we have fine-tuned to a perfect cutting edge.

This process of denial is commonly used when we go to a psychotherapist who does not have the needed training in treating addictions and the effects on the family. When the psychotherapist sees no visible problems, he/she professionally enables the dysfunctional behaviors of the ACoA. We, as ACoAs, then have the professional proof we have been seeking to continue our dysfunctional behaviors.

Another form of distorted reasoning is activated when we say, "I lived with alcoholism all of my life. My father was an alcoholic and I'm smart enough not to let it affect me." The reasoning is, "I survived, so I must be all right." In reality we know that the problems are a direct result of living in a dysfunctional family, but we are afraid of such an admission. If we admit that we were affected, then we must either do something about changing our lives, or continue our lives knowing that we are responsible for what is happening.

ACoAs are masters at masking the problems that we experience. We are very believable in our distortions because we make them look so good. Claudia Black discusses the perfect ACoA smile that covers up dysfunction to the outside world. The smile and good appearance can easily be used as a "con" with therapists who are not aware of such distortions. It is reminiscent of the old Motown song, "Tears of a Clown" — looking so together on the outside and having such pain on the inside.

Gary is an ACoA who had a very dysfunctional family of origin. His father was institutionalized repeatedly and diagnosed as schizophrenic. Gary, marked with pain and distress, stated, "You are trying to have me believe that I'm as crazy as my father. I'm NOT!" Despite multiple assurances that he was not seen as crazy and did not exhibit the same patterns as his father, he would rationalize all of his behavior patterns because of his fear. Gary also used rationalization with the problems that he was experiencing within his marriage and with his children. He would state that his wife was over-reacting or that the problems in the household were not significant. Progress did not occur until Gary was willing to look at his patterns and begin to realize that he wasn't following his father's pattern and nearing institutionalization.

C. COMPARE YOUR WAY OUT

In this denial pattern, we use others to convince ourselves that we don't have a problem. The rationale is, "I can't be an ACoA with problems because there are other people who have it worse than I do." We look for people to use as a comparison who fall under this rationale. A common statement is, "Not only did my sister have it hard growing up, but her marriage is in trouble, and she doesn't go for help."

A Responsible Adult Child, Diane, stated that she was "healthier" than her obese, bulimic sister, Sue. Diane had minimized the effects from her home of origin. Her sister Sue's obesity was more easily noticeable to the onlooker than Diane's dysfunction. As long as Diane used this "comparison" rationalization, her denial and recovery would be permanently hindered.

Step 3: I'm Afraid To Tell You How Mad I Am (Anger)

Auntie Em, boiling internally before the crotchety old Miss Gulch, proposes tying Toto up during the day to appease the wrath of Miss Gulch, but to no avail. Despite her frustration, Auntie Em squelches her feelings of anger by saying that Alvira Gulch doesn't control the whole community just because she holds the majority of its

N

wealth. In total frustration she says, "For 23 years I've been dying to tell you what I thought of you. And now, well, being a Christian woman, I can't say it." Auntie Em denies and stuffs the feelings that are begging to be expressed.

From her statement, Auntie Em has been stifling her anger for over 23 years. It appears that she believes that being Christian (and a woman) does not allow her to get angry and, more importantly, does not allow her to express her anger openly. Most of us avoid anger at all costs. The only family member who appears to have the privilege of expressing anger is the Scapegoat. However, it is generally released in a destructive manner.

We usually handle anger in one of four ways:
(1) by totally denying the feeling;
(2) by pretending it doesn't exist;
(3) by releasing anger destructively, usually at the person(s) we love the most;
(4) by allowing the anger to become internally destructive (i.e., illness, eating disorders, substance abuse).

Dealing with anger is a vital step in the recovery process. As we look at the reality of the effects of alcoholism on our lives, we begin to address the anger which has been submerged for years. This anger must be addressed before recovery can occur.

After five months of therapy, Gladys, a "together"-appearing ACoA, had given herself permission to not only feel, but also to express anger. Her anger emerged from the realization that during her life she had worked on developing socially acceptable survival skills. Now, not only did they not work for her, but she knew exactly when she was using her manipulative gaming skills. Gladys felt as though she had stripped herself of all she was, and believed she got nothing in return except vulnerability. Gladys slowly worked through her anger and began to implement new, healthy behaviors in her life. As she integrated these new skills, Gladys realized that she had kept herself imprisoned, with her anger as her prison bars.

Many of us spend most of our lives either avoiding anger or using anger destructively. The following are four means by which we cause our own destruction:

A. PEACE AT ALL COSTS

When we use this method, we become afraid of anger, believing that its effects will be devastating. Anger is confused with uncontrollable rage. In our home of origin many of us saw destructive anger (actual rage) exhibited by the alcoholic while drinking. Because of these early experiences we avoid all anger with the fear that it will create uncontrollable rage in ourselves and in others. We believe that we can control the anger of others by pleasing people and being good. If someone gets angry, we blame ourselves for not being good enough. Any form of disagreement or disapproval is seen not only as anger, but also as our fault. Because of this, we spend our lives pleasing people, attempting to be perfect and ignoring our own needs in order to keep the peace.

Diane, a member in group therapy, addressed her personal issues as others spoke of their family of origin's "anger expression". Discussion followed on the "scale of anger" which varies in intensity from being mildly disturbed to having intense, uncontrollable rage.

Examples were given of words that describe these feelings in order to show the complete wide range of anger. Diane stated, "I thought all anger was rage." In her family of origin, Diane experienced her alcoholic father expressing only rage and her mother saying nothing. She remembered her mother telling the children that they must be good in order not to provoke their father's rage. Thus her internalized belief was that *she* had the ability to control her father's rage, and consequently everybody else's, by pleasing people and being good. Another message she internalized was that people must express anger in a rageful form. She had spent her life doing anything and everything to avoid anger and then continuously had feelings of guilt and/or resentment.

B. THE TEAKETTLE

Another message that we typically received as children was that we are bad if we feel anger or express that anger. This is typically true for females — we all know that good girls don't get angry. Consequently, we spend our lives justifying our anger and usually never have enough justification for the anger we are feeling. Some self-statements are, "Well. it wasn't that bad", "I can deal with it myself", "It really doesn't matter" or "He must have had a good reason."

Actually anger is stuffed over and over again until we are filled with volcanic anger which blows up at the next person who we feel anger toward. It's like a teakettle that is placed on a stoveburner set on low. Eventually the water gets hotter and hotter and hotter, until it heats up to the point that it blows its whistle. After we release the built-up rage in a destructive manner, we feel guilt and shame. A promise is made to never again have such an inappropriate outburst. The pattern continues over and over again until the built-up anger and rage are released.

C. RAGING VENGEANCE

This method is generally used by the Scapegoat or males who have been given permission to express anger (females generally have not been given permission from

E

society to show or express anger). We learn that the only way to survive and get our needs met is to demand it through anger — which is generally rage. Through this anger, we project onto others the pain we received both physically and emotionally. Instead of saying how much we hurt, we show people our hurt in the only way we know — by displaced anger. The irony is that we not only show our anger to those who have hurt us, but also to those we love, thus pushing those people further away.

D. DISLOYALTY/LOYALTY CONFLICT

In this conflict, denial of anger is seen as a means of loyalty to the family. Statements like, "I can't get angry with them because I love them" or "How can I be angry with Mom? — She has enough problems with Dad" are commonly expressed. We become so enmeshed with the family or with one of our parents that we are not allowed to hurt for ourselves. The overwhelming feelings are guilt and resentment.

Distorted thinking keeps us from talking about the problems and the feelings within our family. The family secret stays locked deep within us through our denial. Although we can clearly see how keeping the secret is hurting the family, telling the secret means being disloyal.

This conflict also occurs during therapy. We disagree or genuinely get angry at the therapist but because of family loyalty (which was built through appreciation), we believe we are not allowed to express our anger. Without taking the risk of expressing anger, we never learn that it is acceptable to express feelings. We also eliminate the knowledge that significant people in our lives will not walk away or ignore us if feelings are expressed.

It is very important to find a therapist who can deal with anger in a positive manner. Learning to express anger in a healthy style is one of the essential keys for the recovery of every ACoA. Therapists need to realize that the anger we express is the anger that has been left unexpressed over a lifetime. This displaced anger is expressed toward the therapist because of the trust held in the therapist, as well as the belief that there will be no negative repercussions. The journey through the anger stage is imperative for movement into the stage of Bargaining.

Step 4: Bargaining for Toto (Bargaining)

Dorothy attempts bargaining with Miss Gulch, explaining that Toto is a defenseless little dog who didn't know he was doing anything wrong. The bargaining intensifies as Dorothy pleads with Miss Gulch, offers to take responsibility for Toto's actions and to receive the consequences. Dorothy states that SHE ALONE was responsible for Toto's entering Miss Gulch's garden and she requests the punishment of going to bed without dinner. Despite Dorothy's valiant attempts, Miss Gulch presents Dorothy with the sheriff's order allowing her to seize the growling dog.

The fourth stage is bargaining. The bargaining stage is where the most elaborate and sophisticated denial patterns take place. This is the stage when we use the phrase, "YES, BUT . . ." when questioned about problems we may be experiencing. "YES, BUT . . ." can take many forms:

A. MINIMIZING

We are minimizing when we make statements like: "My problems aren't that bad", "I know I'm having problems, but . . ." or "This doesn't happen all the time, and besides I know what to do." We view everyone as over-reacting because we are familiar with crises. We feel important when dealing with these crises and we, therefore, minimize the problems that others see us experiencing.

Minimizing is a survival skill we learned while growing up in our family of origin. The fear is that if we really see things the way they are, or if we are as concerned as others, we might not be able to handle the intensity of the situation.

When we minimize, we are plagued with depression and physical problems. This is due to suppressing the feelings that arise as reactions to the events and crises that continually occur. If *we* don't recognize what is happening to us, *our bodies* recognize it for us. We ignore the signals our bodies send us, messages it would be best not to ignore, i.e., headaches, backaches, neck strains, upset stomachs, twitches, shakes, etc.

B. SCAPEGOATING

We use scapegoating when we make statements such as, "I act this way because . . ." or "If it wasn't for . . ." Unfortunately, the most likely scapegoating target is the alcoholic or one of our children in particular. Children are often the focus of the problem because they are easy targets. Parents find that they can avoid their own problems, both personally and within the marriage, by placing the blame on someone else. Children become the targets because of *our* fear of abandonment. Since our

Y

children are the least likely to abandon us, they are the safest targets for blame.

Scapegoating sets the stage for manipulation, game-playing and power struggles. The person(s) who is targeted as the scapegoat(s) is pushed into trying harder to do better and to improve. Unfortunately, nothing is ever good enough. Children learn through family modeling that they need to be perfect. Scapegoating is one of the primary methods of keeping the effects of alcoholism alive in the second generation, even if alcohol isn't present. Children feel responsible for what is taking place within the family and thereafter feel guilty if they can't be perfect. The cycle for the children is continued into adulthood.

Figure 2.1. Vicious Cycle.

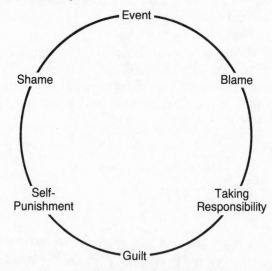

The chart shows the vicious cycle we feel trapped within. First an event occurs, we are blamed and eventually take responsibility for the event. This triggers our guilt and in an attempt to relinquish the guilt, there is self-punishment. When this does not work, we feel shame. Our shame can be exhibited by perfectionism, acting out, isolation or creating a crisis, etc.

It is important to remember that we are under a high level of stress and are moving from one crisis to another. Some of us live in one continuous crisis. The bargaining process is designed to allow us a means to put forth the *minimal* effort necessary to deal with the effects of our problems.

This process has a variety of denial patterns geared at having others, including therapists, put minimal expectations on us. Bargaining becomes increasingly self-defeating when we attempt to compromise or negotiate away unchangeable realities.

The following are some common denial patterns used in the bargaining states:

1. **Compliance:** A person who is complying says, "I'll do whatever you say if you get off my back." Of course we really don't mean what we are saying. What we are actually saying internally is, "I'll never give in to you. I need my control and you are trying to take it away." We think we win by refusing to negotiate.

2. **"Quick Cure":** A "quick cure" occurs when we intellectually believe that we understand the facts, as well as the effects, of alcoholism. We rationalize that we can maintain a healthy lifestyle without pursuing any personal life changes or treatment. The distorted self-message is, "I know too much to ever allow this to affect me." Those of us who use this method convince ourselves, through a nonrational process, that we do not need help. We not only deny the reality of the effects of alcoholism on our lives, but also ignore the need to learn skills in order to have a healthy lifestyle.

3. **Manipulation:** We have been taught how to be master manipulators by our dysfunctional parents. The manipulation skills we learned as children appeared to work at first. However, we notice increasing difficulties with people in adulthood unless we perfect these skills or surround ourselves with people who will allow themselves to be manipulated.

There are two options for continuation of this manipulation: (1) "I'll let you help me if you allow me to have control" or (2) "I'll help you, but you owe me." In the second case each thing that is done has a return debt that will need to be repaid. This is how control is maintained.

There are two last-ditch plans if the above manipulations do not produce the desired effects. These are generally used when the problem is totally overwhelming and we feel like we have lost *all* control. The goal of the pattern is to set ourselves up to lose at the bargaining thus continuing our behaviors. We use these two denial patterns as a process of irrational thinking. This is accompanied by an overwhelming belief that we cannot meaningfully improve our lives and still feel terrified.

a. **The Right to Misery:** We are using "The Right to Misery" manipulation when we say, "I have the right to continue my behaviors even if I feel miserable." This is a very self-destructive stance and there are very few ways that others can reach us when we are in this state. We decide that we have the right to stay unhealthy, but what we are really saying is, "I'm out of control and I don't believe I can regain control, so I might as well convince myself it's okay to stay this way."

b. **Beyond Help:** We not only look and feel hopeless and helpless, but we also let everyone around us know these facts. Our behavior appears to be an open invitation to those around us to help, but we will systematically let each and every person know why their plan will not work. The message given is: "If you try to help me, it will be very difficult for you and besides you will fail anyway." This "beyond help" manipulation keeps us captive and imprisoned within our own pain.

H

Step 5: Hopelessness for Dorothy (Depression)

Dorothy runs into her room and slams the door. She feels totally helpless. With her court order to take away poor Toto, the wicked Miss Gulch has all the power. Dorothy puts her head on the bed, sobbing uncontrollably, as Toto is placed in the basket prison. Dorothy trembles within as she feels the pain and emptiness of being without her beloved friend Toto. Dorothy, in utter despair, feels totally helpless and hopeless!

Figure 2.2. Depression Spiral.

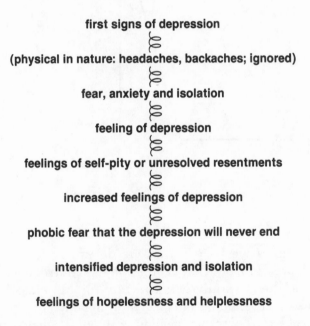

first signs of depression

(physical in nature: headaches, backaches; ignored)

fear, anxiety and isolation

feeling of depression

feelings of self-pity or unresolved resentments

increased feelings of depression

phobic fear that the depression will never end

intensified depression and isolation

feelings of hopelessness and helplessness

Depression occurs when we stuff our feelings and suppress our anger. Most of us are very familiar with depression and, consequently, some of us will seek professional help (initially through a physician). Depression increases as we begin to isolate ourselves, get scared and/or anxious when we feel the beginnings of depression. What happens is similar to a downward spiral.

Figure 2.3a. Dysfunctional Roller-Coaster.

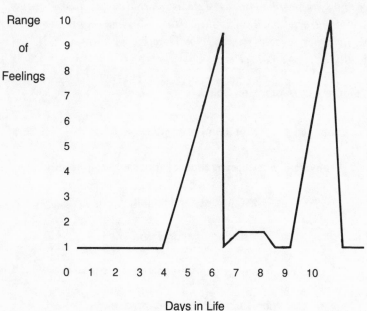

Sometimes we believe that we do not have control over depression, but that depression has control over us. This is the groundwork for feeling hopeless and helpless. Depression is only a symptom which masks the real problem. Therefore, dealing with *just* the depression provides only *temporary* relief and eventually the depression will return.

Another reason the depression continues (besides not taking control of it or not dealing with the feelings) is that we have not yet learned the ordinary range of daily feelings. Life for us has been like living on a roller coaster — up one minute, down the next. Here are two scales, the first Fig. 2.3a. being our dysfunctional roller-coaster life experience and Fig. 2.3b. a healthy life experience.

Figure 2.3b. Healthy Life Experience.

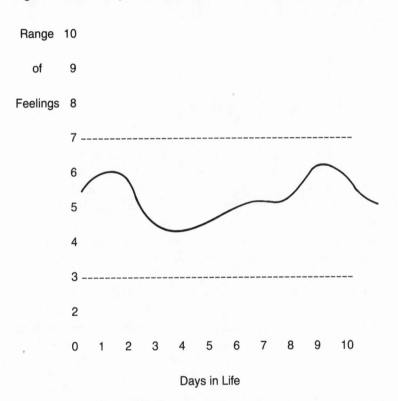

(** The dotted lines show ordinary range)

As illustrated above, the healthy daily feeling range is from 3 to 7, with most days being experienced in that area. Because our days are usually at the extremes when we are dysfunctional, we have very few days that are in the 3 to 7 range. We know when we are going into the extreme range, and it is then that we become anxious and scared. The fear increases and the downward feelings toss us quickly into the lower range of numbers.

When we begin getting healthy and experiencing middle ranges, we initially find it to be "boring and uncomfortable". As we learn we don't *need* crises in our lives, the mid-range becomes more comfortable.

The depression stage may be a result of any of the following:

A. AVOIDANCE OF ANGER

As stated above, many professionals believe that depression is repressed anger. Medication is not a cure-all for depression. Medication is only intended to take the edge off the depression, thereby allowing the person to learn how to control or address the concern. If we don't believe we have the right to feel our anger, it builds into deep resentments. The resentments manifest themselves in forms of depression. Unfortunately, we are plagued with depression because we do not have the skills needed to express anger effectively. Anger management and its personal appropriate expression are essential parts of the recovery process.

B. THE RESPONSIBLE VACATION

The role of being responsible is a high energy role and many times we need a "mental vacation". A Responsible Child cannot justify an actual physical vacation, so a rationalized break may take the form of depression. Being "down" is generally accepted by society as a normal occurrence.

C. LOSS AND GRIEF

We have experienced many losses in our lives and the losses are not just those of dealing with death. There are also the emotional losses of unmet childhood needs, wants and desires. Unfortunately, we have not been taught the skills needed to deal with grief. Society as a whole is unable to deal with the grief process. Many times grief is turned into anger or depression. Without allowing the natural grieving process to happen, depression can be viewed as something to fear. Depression is a *natural part* of the grieving process.

Depression also manifests itself during treatment. During treatment/therapy, we must identify the positive healthy parts we want to keep and the unhealthy parts we desire to change or moderate.

Recall the example of our Responsible Child named Gladys, who felt stripped of her survival skills, totally vulnerable and "naked to the world". If Gladys hadn't expressed her anger, it surely would have been turned into depression. It is vital to learn how to express anger. Perhaps this can better be understood if it is looked at in terms of mourning the old destructive behaviors.

As mentioned earlier, we need to deal with our feelings by sharing them with a counselor and/or someone who has passed through this step. This is a period of high stress and the temptation to deal with stress in old ways is always present. We must give ourselves permission to tell someone how we feel. Because of the temptation to go back to old behaviors, we may use some of the old behaviors occasionally. This does not mean that we have failed! There is no way we can deal with these feelings by ourselves — sharing is a vital element in our journey's success.

During this stage, Steps One, Two and Three of the ACoA self-help group are essential:

1. "Admit we are powerless over the alcoholic and that our lives have become unmanageable."
2. "Come to believe that a Power greater than ourselves can restore us to sanity."
3. "Make a decision to turn our will and our lives over to the care of God as we understand him."

SUMMARY OF OLD PATTERNS

Let's summarize the old patterns that were investigated as we journeyed through our "black and white world". Be aware of these warnings as we enter the doorway to Munchkinland and magnificent Oz.

1. Keep Away By Default: "I don't have time for trivial matters." Diverting attention by downplaying everything.

2. Keep Away By Distraction: "I continue to create crises, and I must be okay because I can handle them." Diverting others' attention from own problems.

3. Overwhelm By Flooding: "I will talk about anything but my problems." Distracting everyone by intellectualizing as if dealing with problems.

4. The Roar of the Lion: "I'll create a mess for you, then I'll fix it to prove you need me." Diverting attention by focusing the attention on others and their problems.

5. Absolutely No: "No, not me. I don't have any problems." Completely denying having any problems.

6. Reasoning the Truth Away: "I know I grew up in a family where there was alcoholism, but it didn't affect me. I've studied this whole thing and I'm not part of this craziness." Rationalization.

M

7. *Compare Your Way Out:* "I don't have as many problems as other members of my family and *they're* not getting help." Diverting by comparing.

8. *Peace At All Costs:* "I can't get angry or something awful will happen." Fearing anger.

9. *The Teakettle:* "I can handle it." Anger building and building and building until it explodes.

10. *Raging Vengeance:* "If you don't do what I say, I'll get angry." Using anger as a mask for pain.

11. *Disloyalty/Loyalty Conflict:* "I can't get angry with them because I love them." Not allowing self to be angry because it will destroy love.

12. *Minimizing:* "My family wasn't that bad and I'm not even sure if alcohol was a problem." Downplaying what is happening.

13. *Scapegoating:* "I only have these problems because of . . ." Diverting by shifting blame to others.

14. *Compliance:* "I'll do anything you say, if you get off my back." Getting rid of others.

15. *Quick Cure:* "I know too much (now that I have the facts) to ever allow this to affect me again." Diverting by flooding self and others with facts.

16. *Manipulation:* "I'll let you help me if you allow me to have control." Attempting to maintain some control in life.

17. *The Right to Misery:* "I have the right to continue my problems even if I feel miserable and go crazy." Refusing help.

18. *Beyond Help:* "If you try to help me, I will make it difficult for you. You will fail anyway." Feeling hopeless and helpless about the situation.

19. *Avoidance of Anger:* "There is nothing to get mad about." Feeling no right to express anger, thus encouraging depression.

20. *The Responsible Vacation:* "I just feel a little down today." Using depression to take a break.

21. *Loss and Grief:* "What do I have to grieve about?" Not dealing with loss and grief issues.

Step 6: This Isn't Kansas Anymore (Acceptance)

The Munchkins cautiously peek out from their hiding place among the lush hollyhocks. Dorothy gazes around the fascinating place in awe. Suddenly, a pink-tinted bubble floats to the ground and bursts to reveal a ravishingly beautiful lady. As Dorothy stares in amazement, she exclaims, "Now I know we're not in Kansas anymore!" Glenda, the beautiful lady in the bubble, nears Dorothy and asks, "Are you a good witch or a bad witch?" Dorothy replies that she is not a witch at all. Nevertheless, she is forced to accept the Ruby Slippers which were once the possession of the Wicked Witch of the East.

The tornado changed Dorothy's life forever. Although she had a long journey ahead of her, she would never return to Kansas the same. All of her thoughts and feelings would be altered and she would see Kansas in a totally different way. Acceptance is the final step — but one that never ends. We are in acceptance when we can look at our destructive behavior without feeling we must create a facade, feel blame, or divert attention. There are three stages of acceptance:

A. IDENTIFYING THE NEGATIVES — IGNORING THE POSITIVES

In this stage we can easily identify the negative/ destructive behaviors while feeling quite uncomfortable in this identification process. When asked for the positives attached to our role(s), we see few if any.

A useful means of pinpointing the positives can be illustrated by the following example: In Beginning Psychoeducational ACoA therapy groups, each member gains an understanding of the roles, and more specifically, his/her own role in the family of origin. The group then identifies the positives and negatives of each role. Therapeutically, it is best to begin with the identification of the positives. The group consistently questions each positive and turns each into a negative. The most uncomfortable time comes when the therapist makes the rule that negatives cannot be discussed. Consistently, group members discuss how difficult it is to hear the positive features of their role. Focusing on the positives appears more uncomfortable for each ACoA than identifying their negative issue. At times, to relieve discomfort after the group identifies the pluses of a particular role, we hear, "Now it's *your* turn, go to the next role."

Be aware that your journey nears this crossroad. You will soon find it is "your turn" . . .

B. SUPERFICIALLY ACCEPTING POSITIVES (WHILE STILL BEING OVERWHELMED BY NEGATIVES)

We seem to accept our positive survival skills only superficially. We have no awareness that these can be used in a healthy manner when working through our unwanted behaviors. We become very impatient with ourselves and want to change everything at once. Then

E

we feel overwhelmed. Because of our de-emphasizing the positives, we see ourselves as vulnerable and as not having any healthy skills. All ACoAs have positive skills but usually don't realize what is hiding within. Remember Dorothy's Ruby Slippers? Although she never realized it, she had held the power to take her self home the whole time.

Soon you will realize the value that you possess inside . . .

C. RECOGNIZING AND ACCEPTING THE POSITIVES

Once we accept our positives we can learn how to use them to our advantage. For example, a Lost Child can feel comfortable spending time by herself. This time can be used for reflection, creativity, personal time and/or meditation. Although in the past it had been used as avoidance, that behavior can now be used in a healthy manner. Another example is that of the Responsible Child who knows how to accept responsibility for others and can now use those same skills in taking care of herself.

Each role has positives. Your life has not been filled with only unhealthy behaviors. Make sure you look at these just as hard as you look at the negatives!

After the Wizard left for Kansas, Glenda appeared before Dorothy and asked what Dorothy had learned. Dorothy replied, "If I ever go looking for something, I must look in my own back yard, because if it's not there . . ." Remember, look in your own "back yard" — there is good within!

We must continually remind ourselves that we do not want to return to the old way of life. We must accept the fact that we have no control over our family of origin, but that the responsibility of our future is with ourselves. *Acceptance can only come to you if you have worked through the other steps, verbalizing your thoughts and feelings each step of the way.*

3

The Journey from Kansas Through Oz

(The Progression and Recovery by Adult Children of Alcoholic Roles)

Glenda sends Dorothy on her way to the border of Munchkinland and then on to the beginning of the magnificent yellow brick road. Dorothy, quite fearful of the journey, exhibits her fear by quickly asking, "But what happens if I . . . ?" Glenda breaks her question in half and assures her that she must "Just follow the yellow brick road." At the edge of the country the Munchkins wave to the hesitant Dorothy as she enters the unknown cornfield.

Dorothy accepts the risk of venturing into the unknown to find her dream. Remember; recovery is a journey, not a destination! Now it is time for you to accept the journey forward. You will meet familiar people along the way. The Wizard, the Wicked Witch, the Scarecrow, the Tin Man and the Cowardly Lion will assist you in your adventure through the Land of Oz. Carefully examine their roles and their accomplishments — it will assist your personal journey.

Author's note: You will soon begin a journey with some familiar characters from Oz. They will be used to illustrate various familial roles. Please be aware that these roles can be combined in many different ways, i.e., Responsible Child and Mascot, Mascot and Lost Child, Responsible Child and Lost Child, etc., to be more expressive of your personalized journey. Use our examples to lead you down your own Yellow Brick Road!

The Scarecrow
(The Responsible Child)

The Scarecrow, dangling from his nail, is perched high above the cornfield. Watching the fields for the farmer is such a thankless job, and being responsible all the time becomes quite taxing, thinks the Scarecrow. The Scarecrow weeps as he describes himself as a total failure. A brain, he declares, would allow him the ability to "unravel every riddle, for any individ'l, in trouble or pain." Continuing as he sings, the Scarecrow declares he would become worthwhile if he only had superior intelligence, and THEN others would love him.

This philosophy epitomizes the life of a Responsible Child in an alcoholic home. The Hero, or Responsible Child, feels "hooked" into the role, unable to escape, just like the Scarecrow. The Responsible Child is the self-imposed caretaker of the family (this is reinforced and encouraged by the family). As Responsible Children, we believe we must solve all of the family concerns. We feel as though we must dedicate our lives to our family and those around us. In fact, after leaving our family of origin, the role of caretaker becomes our purpose in life.

The Responsible Child believes, as did the Scarecrow, that the magic of an external (a brain given to him, a pay raise, a trophy, praise, etc.) will change everything, and thereafter things will be wonderful. This distorted thinking encourages us to continually perform in an attempt to make things wonderful and earn our family's respect and affirmation. The belief is that *we* hold the power to change everything and we *alone* are responsible for those changes. Generally, the means of gaining that respect and self-worth is by overachieving mentally, physically or emotionally for others. This creates a need for perfectionism, rigidity, controlling and workaholism in our attempts to change the world around us.

Common Characteristics of the Responsible Child

• We are usually the firstborn child (may be second child if female, and first child is male)

• We grew up feeling special and now believe that we must continue to correct the imbalance in the family and make up for the family weaknesses

• We dedicate our lives to the family

• We generally keep negative feelings to ourselves (which can lead to resentments and a buildup of anger)

• We have a need for praise (external referencing)

• We always seem to be trying to maintain and uphold the positives to win approval

• We excel physically or mentally, especially in school, sports or work

• We make a physical exit from the family at an early age in pursuit of a distant enterprise or dream

• We stuff our feelings and take on the pain of others

• We give people what they want in an attempt to gain our own rewards

• We often have many health problems, i.e., we are prone to overeating, back pains, etc.

• We have a high rate of heart attacks and strokes

• We hide deep feelings of anger and resentment due to responsible role in the family and feelings of not being appreciated

• We become angry at ourselves for not saying "no" and always putting others first

• We have feelings of loneliness (despite outward signs of acceptance by society)

• We have difficulty with intimacy and relationships

• We usually choose a "helping" profession as a career (i.e., doctor, therapist, nurse, teacher)

• We are generally perfectionists, workaholics

• We may have overspending tendencies

• We have feelings of anger toward parents who many times are critical; we feel as though we don't meet the expectations of parents, and then do not receive approval

- We have feelings of going crazy
- We are good at organizing and doing
- We feel like we must always have the answers
- We can be easily manipulated by co-workers
- We are extremely loyal to those who are disloyal to us
- We accept crises as frequent and normal parts of our lives
- We have a large number of projects going at one time and overextend ourselves

Although the Responsible Child most generally assumes the Enabler role after marriage, we are going to look at this role as it develops from childhood into adulthood. Throughout our lives, we have continued our role of being responsible. There are some of us, however, who have changed to another role at some point in our lives. Most likely, the change happened as a result of a severe trauma. The trauma was something that totally devastated us into believing that we could no longer hold the role of being responsible. Another reason for a role change occurs when identical roles marry. This forces one of the two to assume a new role. For those of us who have changed our roles due to a trauma, we still have positives from our original role. The number of positives we have obtained from this role depends on the age the trauma occurred. For others of us, we periodically retake our role, thus regaining the positives. The reason that we have difficulty looking at our positives as Responsible Children is fourfold.

1. Negatives are seen as the key to fixing situations.
2. The struggle for perfection is constant.
3. A protection device is a safety net.
4. Old messages received by the family of origin are ingrained.

Let's look at each factor.

Y

A. NEGATIVES ARE SEEN AS THE KEY TO FIXING

When a problem occurs in a dysfunctional family, it is viewed as the "job" of the Responsible Child to fix it by being responsible. As Responsible Children we have been taught that if something goes wrong, we should take charge of the situation and fix it, whether or not it's our problem. *Every* problem becomes *our* problem.

For example, as a Responsible Child in an alcoholic family, we attempt to alter the behaviors of our parents by our own behavior. Our thoughts include, "If only I didn't . . ." or "If only I did this, Mom and Dad wouldn't have got into an argument," or "She's in a bad mood, don't upset her." Instead of realizing that we don't have control over our family or our drinker, we focus on what we see ourselves doing to cause the problems. Even if our alcoholic becomes sober, we truly believe that we have the responsibility to help our nonalcoholic parent keep the alcoholic sober. We walk on eggshells, attempting to be as good as possible. We become more responsible and treat the alcoholic like a china doll. Ultimately, we treat the recovering member as if he/she is ready to break at any moment if *we* are not there to help protect him/her. This distorted thinking is like attempting to drive a car by only using the horn, and then wondering why it doesn't go where we want it to go. This sets up a pattern of continuous self-blame and a belief that one person can control another.

B. THE CONSTANT STRUGGLE FOR PERFECTION

As Responsible Children, we believe that we can compensate for the behaviors of others by being perfect. Because of this belief, we focus on how we are *not* perfect, hoping to get the formula for perfection. We also believe that we are not allowed to give ourselves credit for anything. The only thing that really counts is reaching "the goal". This is like climbing a mountain, with the only measure of success being to reach the top. If we do not reach the top, we see ourselves as a total failure. However, even if we reach the top, we minimize the accomplishment or we are already planning how we need to climb the next mountain. We never allow ourselves the pleasures of our accomplishments.

The following illustrates this all too vividly:

THE STATION

By Robert J. Hastings

Tucked away in our subconscious minds is an idyllic vision. We see ourselves on a long, long trip that almost spans the continent. We're traveling by passenger train, and through the windows we drink in the passing scene of cars on nearby highways, of children waving at a crossing, of cattle grazing on a distant hillside, of smoke pouring from a power plant, of row upon row of corn and wheat, of flatlands and valleys, of mountains and rolling hillsides, of city skylines and village halls, of biting winter and blazing summer and cavorting spring and docile fall.

But uppermost in our minds is the final destination. On a certain day at a certain hour we will pull into the station. There will be bands playing and flags waving. And once we get there, so many wonderful dreams will come true. So many wishes will be fulfilled and so many pieces of our lives finally will be neatly fitted together like a completed jigsaw puzzle. How restlessly we pace the aisles damning the minutes for loitering . . . waiting, waiting, waiting for the station.

However, sooner or later we must realize there is no station, no one place to arrive at once and for all. The true joy of life is the trip. The station is only a dream. It constantly outdistances us.

"When we reach the station, that will be it!" we cry. Translated it means, "When I'm 18, that will be it! When I put the last kid through college, that will be it! When I win a promotion, that will be it! When I reach the age of retirement, that will be it! I shall live happily ever after!"

Unfortunately, once we get "it", then "it" disappears. The station somehow hides itself at the end of an endless track.

"Relish the moment" is a good motto, especially when coupled with Psalm 118:24, "This is the day which the Lord hath made; we will rejoice and be glad in it." It isn't the burdens of today that drive men mad. Rather, it is regret over yesterday or fear of tomorrow. Regret and fear are twin thieves who rob us of today.

So stop pacing the aisles and counting the miles. Instead, climb more mountains, eat more ice cream, go barefoot oftener, swim more rivers, watch more sunsets, laugh more and cry less. Life must be lived as we go along. The station will come soon enough.

C. PROTECTION DEVICE

Despite the destructive characteristics of our over-responsibility, caretaking and fixing behaviors, we continue to believe that we must do everything at all costs. Because we see ourselves as pillars of strength, needing to have all the answers, we believe it is our duty to fix problems. We feel it is necessary to hide our personal imperfections. We believe we must conquer our imperfections without any help from others or we have failed. We draw our strength from helping others and not helping ourselves. We assume that we will be seen as irresponsible if others see how much we hurt. If they see our pain, they will realize how phony we have been, because we really *do not* have an answer for everything. They can never know that *we* have a need to be supported and not always worry about someone else.

D. OLD MESSAGES RECEIVED BY THE FAMILY OF ORIGIN

We were all given messages as children from our parents. We became what our parents directly told us we "are" or "are not". Many of our messages came from what was said nonverbally (the family rules that were never stated orally but were *just known*). One example is

L

the message about sex. Usually we were not told, but we knew exactly how our parents felt about sex and especially how we were expected to behave.

We learned through our "shame-based family" our family's rules. When we were disciplined, our parents usually said, "*You* are bad for doing _____!" instead of saying that it was the *behavior* that was bad. This gave us the message that we were bad as a person, thus continuing our shame.

Other messages given to us while growing up were: "We won't accept anything but the best from you. We know you can do it!" (setup for perfection); "We depend on you to help us!" (pressure to fix things) and, "You should know better because you are the oldest!" (pressure to know everything just because of age).

These are just a few messages we received as children. After we left our family of origin, it was almost as if our parents (usually one parent more than the other) were sitting on our shoulders directing every move and telling us our every mistake. Shame and guilt were used to embed these messages into our being, and we feel shame when we go against a message that was repeatedly instilled in us.

The Positive Side of the Responsible Child

The Scarecrow stands anxiously before the Wizard awaiting his promised brain. The Wizard says, to the Scarecrow's amazement, "You've had it all the time," as he hands the Scarecrow a parchment containing a ThD (a Doctorate of Thinkology). As the Scarecrow rattles off mathematical formulas, he realizes he always had the power within.

A "brain" is but one part of the positive attributes of the Responsible Child. Contrary to popular belief, there are numerous positive behaviors that need to be identified. These positive behaviors are essential to the integration process of recovery. Awareness gives us stability in the knowledge that we have important ingredients within ourselves for personal recovery. We discover that we don't have to throw out every part of our old selves and begin molding a whole new self.

Before you read on, write down the positives that have been developed and learned as a result of this role. It doesn't matter if this is your role or not. Look at the strengths of the role. (Please do not feel limited by the numbering.)

1 _____	8 _____
2 _____	8 _____
3 _____	10 _____
4 _____	11 _____
5 _____	12 _____
6 _____	13 _____
7 _____	14 _____

HERE ARE SOME OF YOUR POSITIVES

THE RESPONSIBLE CHILD . . .

is organized
is self-reliant
has high stress tolerance
is an excellent student
has leadership qualities
makes decisions
is a good listener
pays attention to details
is mature for age
is introspective
can accomplish most
    anything
has self-control
wants to do the best job
honors commitments
is spiritual
is very energetic
implements ideas
finishes tasks
is popular with peers
is sensitive to others
is responsible
is fashion-conscious
is competitive
is thrifty

is self-motivating
is punctual (usually early)
is loyal
is compassionate
follows orders
trusts self with tasks
is excellent in a crisis
is a high achiever
is very logical/reasonable
is dependable
is an excellent volunteer
has stamina
follows rules
has high morals
is active in the community
can take over at once
has a good memory
is highly intellectual
gives good directions
is meticulous
is tenacious
is admired or even envied
is a hard worker
is honest
gets results

Because of these strengths, the Responsible Child chooses careers that are in the helping professions. These careers include teachers, nurses, counselors, doctors, lawyers, social workers, office managers, senators and even President of the United States. Some Responsible Children choose other careers based not on the interaction with people, but the responsibility of the career.

E

Place within this diploma the positives that you possess from this role. Include with an asterisk (*) the characteristics you desire to integrate into your journey.

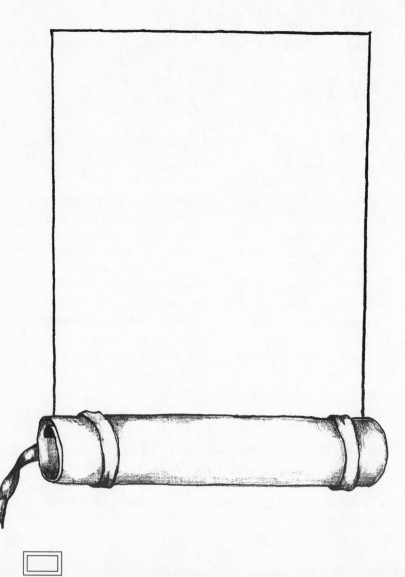

The Progression and Recovery of the Responsible Child

Cautiously the Scarecrow enters the magnificent castle in the Emerald City. Closer and closer he inches toward the fiery powerful magnificent Oz. The journey has been difficult but amazingly rewarding. The foursome have successfully destroyed the cruel Wicked Witch, but hesitantly the Scarecrow awaits his final unknown challenge . . .

As Responsible Children, our progression into the role is marked by an intense sense of frustration which develops from unrealistic expectations, over-responsibility, controlling, recurrent unmet needs, deceit, pain and anger. By the time we have progressed to the point of crisis, we are plagued by chronic depression and feelings of helplessness. Our depression is similar to a black, ominous raincloud that is always over our heads like the one following the Al Capp character, Joe Btfsplk. We have spent our entire lives trying to control everything around us, including our depression. We constantly try to control the feelings within us, but to no avail. Exhausted by our failures in the quest for perfection, we become physically incapable of maintaining control for one moment longer. Unsuccessful at meeting our goals, we fall deeper and deeper into depression. To hide our pain and anguish, we begin to numb more of our feelings to protect our very being. A desperately tired Barb stated in therapy, "I must have control or I'll go crazy! The more I feel out of control, the more I try to gain control. Through processing, I realize that it's the control that makes me feel crazy, not the lack of it!" This sense of complete helplessness causes us to "hit bottom" and seek assistance with our journey.

Looking at the Progression and Recovery Chart of the Responsible Child, (Figure 3.1), we see that the recovery for the Responsible Child is quite erratic in nature. The up-down cycle is quite predictable, with its sharp jumps and declines. Note that the sharpness of the jumps decrease as recovery increases. As we progress in our recovery, we find that our relapses are shorter in duration and frequency as we learn skills to address our detoured journey forward.

At the point of crisis, or "bottoming out", we immediately try to learn as much as possible about our role, the effects of that role, and the characteristics we manifest. It is almost as if we are consumed with gaining the information quickly and becoming the master so we can move on to the next challenge. Somehow, we believe this "recovery thing" should be accomplished in a month or so! Of course, this "recovery thing" (the journey) must be mastered now so we can get ready for our next project!

In the early recovery stages we try to attack all of our issues at one time — the controlling, lack of intimacy, the frozen feelings, over-responsibility, etc. Alas, our journey is quite superficial at this point. Our journey up the Yellow Brick Road is for *others* (family, spouse, parents, etc.) but not for *ourselves*. We are so conditioned to fix things and do for others that we see no other choices along the path.

Once we realize that our journey has been for others, we make dramatic progress as we struggle to make the journey for ourselves. We learn to "chunk down" concerns and take small steps toward our recovery. We learn that this process is the only real method to deal with our issues successfully. The overwhelming fears tend to lessen as we discover that we need to take small steps and look at our progress. The controlling issues and over-responsibility seem to be the first steps that many of us address early in our journey toward recovery.

It should be noted that up to this point we seem to change our behaviors by doing almost the extreme

A

opposite. If we are overly responsible with the children, we think that the answer is to turn all responsibility over to our spouse or turn it over to our children. There seems to be no gradual turnover, no gentle grey area of change. We tend to go from "black to white" as a means of problem-solving. Obviously for the progression in our journey, it is imperative that we learn early in our program the skills of decision-making, value clarification and the change process.

Many times we find that the payoffs for change are not worth the emotional turmoil involved in the process. This is indicated in the Figure 3.1 by the arrows that point to the right. This indicates a backslide in recovery or a discontinuation of our journey. At other points along the way, we tend to level off and move in a straight line before we journey onward — this is a relapse in our progression.

As we continue in recovery, we may become plagued with "out-of-control" feelings. A highly sensitive Adult Child named Pat remarked, "Trusting and opening up to my husband was like walking around naked. I know that he knows the 'secrets', but I'm so scared and fearful of what he'll see!"

The graph, as well as the step-by-step expanded format for recovery, is a flexible working stepping stone. Use it as a guide for your journey. Remember that each person's journey may not take him/her down identical paths — each of us are individuals and may not address every issue at the same time or have exactly the same program for recovery.

As we forge ahead it appears that each new core issue brings new fears of going forward. Because of our "readiness factor", our skills, feelings, anger and losses must be re-addressed over and over again. Recovery is challenging, but the progression into the future is filled with hope, happiness and adventure. This journey can be a change that makes a lifetime difference.

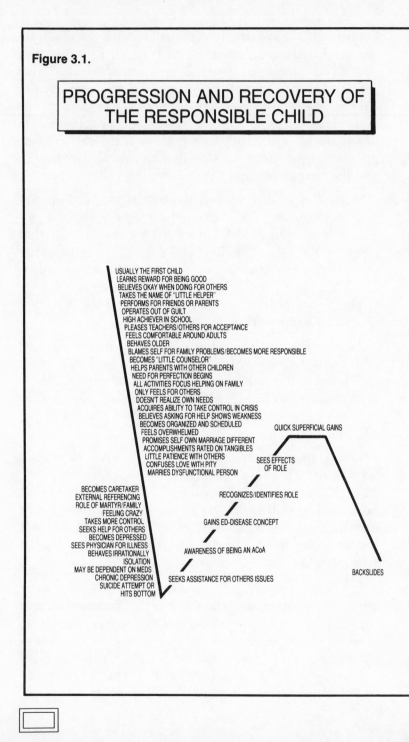

Figure 3.1.

PROGRESSION AND RECOVERY OF THE RESPONSIBLE CHILD

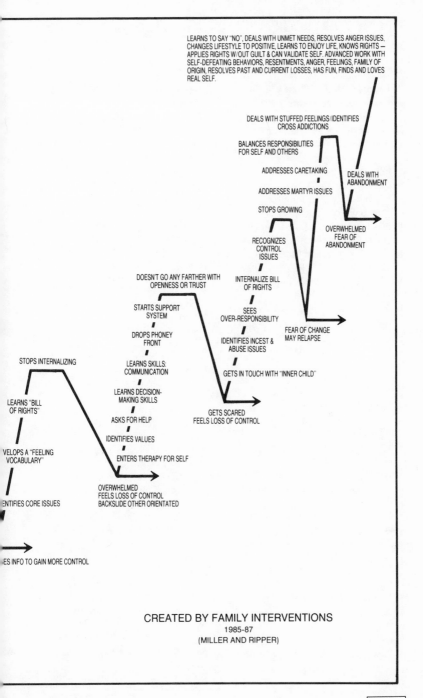

LEARNS TO SAY "NO", DEALS WITH UNMET NEEDS, RESOLVES ANGER ISSUES, CHANGES LIFESTYLE TO POSITIVE, LEARNS TO ENJOY LIFE, KNOWS RIGHTS — APPLIES RIGHTS W/OUT GUILT & CAN VALIDATE SELF. ADVANCED WORK WITH SELF-DEFEATING BEHAVIORS, RESENTMENTS, ANGER, FEELINGS, FAMILY OF ORIGIN, RESOLVES PAST AND CURRENT LOSSES, HAS FUN, FINDS AND LOVES REAL SELF.

DEALS WITH STUFFED FEELINGS/IDENTIFIES CROSS ADDICTIONS

BALANCES RESPONSIBILITIES FOR SELF AND OTHERS

ADDRESSES CARETAKING

DEALS WITH ABANDONMENT

ADDRESSES MARTYR ISSUES

STOPS GROWING

OVERWHELMED FEAR OF ABANDONMENT

RECOGNIZES CONTROL ISSUES

DOESN'T GO ANY FARTHER WITH OPENNESS OR TRUST

INTERNALIZE BILL OF RIGHTS

STARTS SUPPORT SYSTEM

SEES OVER-RESPONSIBILITY

DROPS PHONEY FRONT

FEAR OF CHANGE MAY RELAPSE

IDENTIFIES INCEST & ABUSE ISSUES

LEARNS SKILLS: COMMUNICATION

LEARNS DECISION-MAKING SKILLS

GETS IN TOUCH WITH "INNER CHILD"

STOPS INTERNALIZING

ASKS FOR HELP

IDENTIFIES VALUES

GETS SCARED FEELS LOSS OF CONTROL

LEARNS "BILL OF RIGHTS"

ENTERS THERAPY FOR SELF

VELOPS A "FEELING VOCABULARY"

OVERWHELMED FEELS LOSS OF CONTROL BACKSLIDE OTHER ORIENTATED

ENTIFIES CORE ISSUES

ES INFO TO GAIN MORE CONTROL

CREATED BY FAMILY INTERVENTIONS
1985-87
(MILLER AND RIPPER)

STEP-BY-STEP PROGRESSION OF THE RESPONSIBLE CHILD

1. Learns within the first year how to manipulate parents and significant others.
2. Learns during second year that if he/she does something for parents or is good, there is a high reward — attention.
3. Believes he/she is okay only when doing something for someone or being "good".
4. Has intense need for parents to say "I love you".
5. Takes the name of Mommy's or Daddy's "Little Helper".
6. Performs for friends of parents.
7. Operates out of guilt.
8. Begins to fill role of caretaker for siblings.
9. High achiever in school.
10. Pleases teachers and others for acceptance.
11. Feels comfortable around adults — behaves older than age.
12. Either blames self for problems in family or becomes more responsible.
13. Listens to parents' problems — "Little Counselor".
14. Helps parents control other children — learns to give orders and directions.
15. Needs perfection in life to gain strokes.
16. Wants to be the best — average is not good enough.
17. All activities focus on helping the family or family image.
18. Can only feel for others and doesn't recognize own needs.
19. Acquires ability to take control in crisis.
20. Competes with siblings to be #1.
21. Believes that asking for help shows weakness.
22. Becomes very organized and scheduled.
23. Resents siblings for not helping out.
24. Feels overwhelmed.
25. Promises self that things will be different in own marriage.
26. Accomplishments rated on tangibles.
27. Has little patience with others.
28. Confuses love and pity — chooses someone he/she can pity and take care of for a mate.
29. Marries a dysfunctional person and takes on a mothering role/caretaking continues.
30. Self-esteem based on opinions of others.
31. Takes role of martyr in family.
32. Activities center on controlling the dysfunctional person.
33. Feelings of going crazy.
34. Attempts to take more control.
35. Seeks help for dysfunctional person.
36. Feels everyone is working against him/her.
37. Stress-related illnesses.
38. Becomes depressed.
39. Contacts physician for depression, but believes it is other people's lack of help that is the root of the problem.
40. Begins behaving irrationally.
41. Isolation (physically and emotionally).
42. Chronic depression.
43. May become dependent on prescribed medication or alcohol (more likely eating disorders, workaholism, over-spending).
44. Suicide attempt or hits personal bottom.

STEP-BY-STEP RECOVERY OF THE RESPONSIBLE CHILD

1. Awareness of being an ACoA.
2. Seeks assistance for issues of others (ie, spouse, children).
3. Gains education on family disease concept, ACoA issues, etc.
4. Recognition/identification of role played in family of origin.
5. Recognition/identification of present day role and effects of that role.
6. Quick, superficial therapeutic gain, motivation for recovery high.
7. Identifies ACoA core issues.
8. Develops a "feeling" vocabulary.
9. Overwhelmed with issues, feels loss of control.
10. Black/white dealings with core issues.
11. Backslide, other-oriented.
12. Enters therapy for self.
13. Asks for help.
14. Learns communication skills, decision-making and values clarification.
15. Starts to drop phoney front/still has difficulty asking for help.
16. Starts to set up a support system, may join ACoA group.
17. Considers bringing children into therapy.
18. Gets scared with opening up and trusting; feels loss of control.
19. Gets in touch with "child" inside.
20. Identifies incest and abuse issues.
21. Recognizes over-responsibility.
22. Fear of change, may relapse.
23. Recognizes control issues/begins to let go selectively and reluctantly.
24. Fear of change, may relapse.
25. Recognizes caretaking, martyr personality and its destructiveness.
26. Begins to allow others to take responsibility for themselves to some degree.
27. Fear of anger, scared of awareness or insight in self and significant others.
28. Identifies cross addiction (compulsive loving, over-eating, over-spending, drug abuse).
29. Begins to deal with "stuffed" feelings.
30. Feels overwhelmed, fears loss of control.
31. Possible relapse — fear of abandonment.
32. Deals with abandonment issues, anger, hurt, fears.
33. Deals with people-pleasing, identifies some boundaries.
34. Identifies unmet needs past and present.
35. Learns to say "no".
36. Learns to ask for needs to be met.
37. Clarifies personal choicemaking.
38. Gains accuracy in identification of feelings.
39. Recognition/identification of personal anger issues.
40. Identification of old messages.
41. Brings children into therapy.
42. Clarifies present issues.
43. Recognition/identification of personal loss and grief issues, past and present.
44. Identification of distorted thinking and hearing processes.
45. Learns process of "change structure"/clarifies boundaries.
46. Advanced work with self-defeating behaviors.
47. Begins to accept the "child" inside.
48. Advanced work with fears of abandonment, hurt, fear, anger.

49. Identifies need not to set up crisis.
50. Sets own personal "bill of rights"/appropriate needs attainment.
51. Addresses people-pleasing behaviors.
52. Becomes more assertive.
53. Learns to set limits with others.
54. Recognizes unrealistic expectations of self and others.
55. Starts to find healthy friends, minimizes unhealthy friendships.
56. Identification of external referencing.
57. Looks once again at personal needs left unmet.
58. Identifies and clarifies resentments, anger.
59. Pulls away from unhealthy family member, shares with other family members in home of origin.
60. Advanced work on anger; fearful of loss of all control.
61. Advanced work on sexual or incest issues/abuse.
62. Learns relaxation techniques, meditation.
63. Accepts the "child" inside.
64. Mourns loss of old person; advanced grief and loss work.
65. Integrates spirituality.
66. Gives self permission to have fun, takes risks with self.
67. New interests develop.
68. Experiences positive "self" feelings/more self-affirming.
69. Increased self-worth, self-esteem.
70. Finds the "new person" integrated inside.
71. Decides if spouse is wanted in therapy or spouse wants to go into therapy.
72. Ability to identify <u>and</u> ask for fulfillment of needs from family and significant others.
73. Deals with relationship issues, intimacy issues, parenting issues.
74. Family ties become healthier.
75. Gives self permission to be happy and set personal goals.
76. Sets family goals.
77. Breaks cycle.

THERAPEUTIC ISSUES

Therapy must be done in a slow, gradual, step-by-step method for the development of trust. Confrontational methods that are commonly used with active alcoholics are ineffective and typically bring out Adult Children's defenses in therapy. To the therapists' disbelief, much time is spent protecting the Adult Child's territory or thoughts when confrontation is attempted. Our intellectualizations and rationalizations can be addressed, however, if done in a loving, supportive manner. When we develop the belief that we will not be shamed by the therapist, we begin to look at the confrontations not as threats, but as evaluation of distorted thinking which developed from our homes of origin. It is important that we develop this rapport with the therapist early in therapy so we can establish the groundwork for allowing our feelings to surface in a safe environment. Without that trust in the therapist and the belief in the safety of our journey, we will be fearful of the unknown path. As Responsible Children, we must be taught to "get out of our heads" and "deal with our hearts" in the journey.

Due to our needs for mastery, we need hands-on materials in therapy. This gives us a practical, down-to-earth, step-by-step approach to evaluate our progress. Psychoeducational methods are *essential* because we have missed many valuable learning skills from our dysfunctional homes of origin. To our surprise, we find many areas that need to be learned or readjusted for our progress. Change is frightening for us because we feel as though we are losing survival techniques that have always worked for us in the past. Many of our old dysfunctional ways of thinking and behaviors feel almost like old friends that we hate to lose or modify.

The "Progression and Recovery" charts, as well as the "Step-by-Step" sheets, set up a type of self-administered treatment plan for our recovery program. The skills we attain become our safeguard along our "pilgrimage". "Pilgrimage" is a perfect word for our therapeutic endeavor as it is defined as "a journey held in reverence or honor". Our journey is a trip of reverence and honor because we are in search of the greatest gift of all — love of self!

The Wicked Witch
(The Scapegoat)

The Wicked Witch rejoices as the captured Dorothy trembles, listening to the threatening promise of her friends' impending death. The terrifying Witch declares that the shaking Scarecrow will be the first victim. The Witch cackles as the onlookers' terror encompasses the tower courtyard. The life-threatening fire comes closer and closer to the shivering Scarecrow. The only sound is the terrifying screech of the Witch's laughter . . .

In every fairy tale there must be a bad guy, evil-doer or wicked witch. So, too, is the need for a bad guy or "scapegoat" in each dysfunctional family, without whom, it appears the drama could not have meaning or continuation.

As Scapegoats, we feel trapped in the role of wearing the family black hat. Without our existence, however, someone else would move into the antagonist role. When the Wicked Witch of the West died, her sister, the Wicked Witch of the East, took over the reign of terror.

Contrast the Wicked Witch of the East to Glenda, the Good Witch — it's a stark, night-and-day difference. Everything that makes up the structure of the Good Witch is the complete opposite makeup of the Wicked Witch. This analogy perfectly exemplifies what occurs in the progression of the family Scapegoat's role. The Scapegoat is the complete opposite of the Responsible Child. Interestingly enough, the Scapegoat desires the "strokes" gained by the Responsible Child and the Responsible Child desires the adventure and fun enjoyed by the Scapegoat.

Common characteristics of the Scapegoat

• We are generally the second child in the family order (unless male is first child and replaced by next order-of-

N

birth child which is a daughter who takes on the responsible role.)

- We feed on negative attention due to inability to gain positives
- We have a high degree of alcohol or drug use/abuse
- We have a high rate of criminal involvement
- We have a high rate of DUI offenses
- We have a high rate of car accidents, vandalism, shoplifting
- We generally lead hazardous lifestyles with high rates of abortions, addiction and risk-taking episodes
- We are attracted to others who act out
- We build a strong wall of defense to keep others out
- We desperately care, but hide our need for love, caring and concern
- We have a high rate of suicides
- We feel lonely, rejected, hurt, angry
- We are full of rebellion and defiance
- We move the focus of the family away from the addicted person
- We have a high rate of pregnancy, early sexual activity and early marriage
- We lack skills needed to maintain an honest, open, intimate relationship
- We have an inner need to be understood and to find someone who believes in us
- We have a high rate of job switching and job loss
- We often switch to a Hero role in recovery

"The Scapegoat has positives? Never!!!" This philosophy is held by everyone, even the Scapegoat. There is a fourfold reason the Scapegoat does not identify with the positives of their role.

1. The family has a need for a Scapegoat.
2. There are old messages from the dysfunctional family of origin.
3. A protection device is used.
4. Giving up seems to be the only option left.

A. The Family's Need for a Scapegoat

The Scapegoat's characteristics and behaviors allow the family a means of diverting attention away from the family problems. This is accomplished by shifting the negative focus onto the Scapegoat. The family does not allow the Scapegoat to have any positives. If our family recognizes our positives, we wouldn't be the Scapegoat any longer. No one else in the family wants our distasteful role, so they become experts at shifting the blame or diverting attention to us. It's like a hot potato that everyone is constantly tossing at us.

Another important lesson that we learn through repetition is one in "family reunification". We learn very quickly that if we cause problems in our family, our parents will stop fighting and start working together to take care of the problems.

Tina is a very astute eight year old. Her parents are divorced and she lives with her alcoholic father and her stepmother. She is the youngest of three children and has been given the Scapegoat role in her family. Although her stepmother came into therapy initially because of Tina's father's chronic alcoholism, Tina was quickly cited as one of the major problems within the family. The family and the school wanted Tina in therapy to "fix" her behavioral problems. After meeting with Tina several times, she confided, "If I'm bad, my stepmother and dad stop fighting and they pay attention to me. I'm afraid that they will kill each other (father had physically abused stepmother and would throw sharp objects at her). I *can* stop them just by doing something bad."

Tina was a very sensitive child who was starving for love and affection. She talked regularly about her concerns for her alcoholic father and her drug-abusing mother. She reported feeling loved at times by her stepmother, but stated that she realized her stepmother was busy taking care of Tina's dad — and Tina's dad was more in need than Tina.

One day while meeting with the entire family, Tina's dad became very upset. He reported that his ex-wife was in a diabetic coma due to her use of drugs and her neglect to take her insulin. Tina began sobbing and when her dad was asked to comfort her, he stated in a gruff voice, "Why should I? It's *my* ex-wife! And besides Tina has been bad today and does not deserve anything." Tina instantly stopped crying and put on her tough exterior facade of having no feelings.

This situation is not uncommon for Scapegoats. When we show our feelings, we are verbally annihilated by the ones we most want to love us. Thus we learn not to show what we feel, especially not in a vulnerable manner. We learn to build around us protective walls which are cemented with our tears of pain.

B. Old Messages from the Dysfunctional Family of Origin

Our old messages are negative and consistent. Some of these messages are, "You can't do anything right"; "I can't trust you any further than I can see you"; "This family wouldn't have any problems if it wasn't for you"; "I'm afraid to answer the phone because I know it's someone telling me about something you have done" or "Can't you be good just for a day?"

The life of the Scapegoat becomes one of self-fulfilling prophecy. Someone once said, "You are what others say you are, and you are not what others say you are not." We learn to become what our families have ingrained in our memories — to be bad! It has been proven that if you take a "normal", healthy child and place that child in an institution with mentally and emotionally disturbed children, that child will not only behave the same as the other children, but he will also soon see himself as disturbed. (This can also happen in unhealthy work places.) The same thing happens to the Scapegoat. We

G

are told we are bad, so we behave and see ourselves as bad.

Richard is a 17 year old who has lived through his mother's four divorces, as well as her alcoholism. His mother and stepfather were coming in for marriage counseling and Richard was identified as one of the major concerns in their marriage. When meeting with Richard, he stated, "Why should I change? My mother tells everyone how bad I am; I would hate to disappoint her." During that session Richard also said, "You are going to work at having me feel! You don't understand — I can't afford to feel. If I feel, it would mean dealing with all the hurt and anger that I have worked all these years to ignore!"

This is not an uncommon response for those of us who are Scapegoats. We get the message that we will ALWAYS be bad. We submit, and then need to become numb to avoid the pain that accompanies the "bad" role. Our defenses become stronger and stronger as we become imprisoned by our own anger and pain.

C. The Protection Device

One law of nature is that when an animal is trapped or backed into a corner, it fights to get out. It will use any technique possible to escape. So, too, will the Scapegoat. As Scapegoats we fight in an attempt to save ourselves from the pain and, at times, fight for our very lives. From this struggle come the positives that the family never sees. The family never sees underneath the fighting. The family never sees our desire to "be good" or the hurt and pain we truly hold within. The family is too busy passing us hot potatoes.

D. Giving Up

After years of fighting and hoping the family will let up or see some good in us, we resign ourselves to the role. We feel we have no other choice but to be the way our family wants us to be. So we spend our time and energy perfecting and living the role.

THE POSITIVE SIDE OF THE WICKED WITCH

Dorothy quickly picks up the bucket of water to save the Scarecrow from his impending fiery death. Dorothy flings the contents of the bucket, misdirecting it onto the Wicked Witch as she screams in agony. "You cursed brat! What have you done?" The Witch yells as she shrivels and melts before the amazed onlookers. Everyone stands in silent astonishment as the Witch becomes a melted, bubbling pool on the castle floor.

How can the Scapegoat have any positives? If the Witch was not so wicked, our foursome would not have found their inner strengths. We give others in the family a means of finding strength within themselves. Our reward, when we act out, is watching the family pull together in times of crises. We feel useful and worthy in assisting the family, even if this feeling is self-destructive. With a little guidance, however, we can learn skills to attain positive affirmation in a much less self-destructive manner.

Before you read on, write down the positives that have been developed and learned as a result of this role. It doesn't matter if this is your role or not. Look at the strengths of the role. (Please do not feel limited by the numbering.)

1 _____   4 _____

2 _____   5 _____

3 _____   6 _____

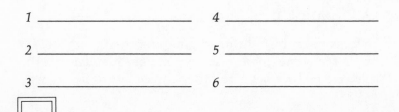

HERE ARE SOME OF YOUR POSITIVES

THE SCAPEGOAT . . .

is spontaneous

is easygoing

is always able to pull through

gets needs met

is loyal to friends

is open — doesn't keep family secrets

knows how to have fun

has sensitivity to others (masked)

is compassionate (with people who allow it)

is efficient — finds short cuts

is a good listener (to people who will confide in them)

has hidden talents

is good in a crisis

is protective of friends

is energetic

is adaptable

has a quick wit

is flexible

speaks up for self

is self-motivating (outside family)

lives in the present

is emotional (inside, never shown)

is emotionally strong

has leadership qualities

is mechanically inclined

has a diverse personality

is a good negotiator

is assertive

has a good memory

loves challenges

forms long-lasting relationships

is a quick thinker

takes risks

is excitement oriented

is creative

is attuned to people

is physically strong

E

Place within this witch's hat the positives that you possess from this role. Include with an asterisk (*) the characteristics you desire to integrate into your journey.

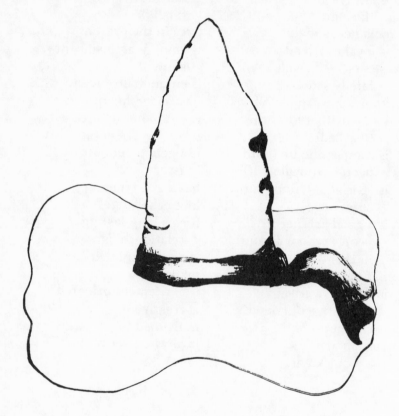

We may still have difficulty owning up to these positive behaviors. Our family, on the other hand, may have a lot of difficulty believing these positives are true. Remember, it's that lack of positive vision that *forms the role* for the Scapegoat.

Some Scapegoats choose jobs which allow mobility and are short-term in nature so they can arrange their own hours. Some have a history of changing jobs frequently. Others of us use our feelings as motivators and become hard-working employees and employers. Common jobs for the Scapegoat are those of salesmen, construction workers, bartenders, insurance agents, race car drivers, parachutists, soldiers, policemen, firemen, collection agents, pilots, maintenance workers, handymen, self-employed workers, mechanical workers, etc.

The Progression and Recovery of the Scapegoat

Confused about the commotion around her, Dorothy explains that her farmhouse, which fell from the sky, was not an unexplained miracle. Dorothy unsuccessfully attempts to convince the doubtful Munchkins that her killing of the Wicked Witch was just an accident of sorts. "It was just a coincidence," she tells the tiny people of Oz. Although Dorothy is bewildered by her inability to convince the Munchkins, they proceed to sing the praises of the joyous news — the Wicked Witch of the East is absolutely . . . positively . . . dead! Jubilation continues as the unknowing Munchkins naively think that the death of the Wicked Witch will end all of their woes.

Progression into the role of Scapegoat is painful. Our means of survival is very risky because Scapegoats thrive on negative attention. The Responsible Child is jealous of us because he/she thinks we have too much fun and get away with too much.

Our progression is marked by denial. Our denial is hard to break and can lead to termination of concern from others who don't understand our need to battle the process. We are scared children trapped within a rebellious facade! Our frustration, hurt and anger drive others away.

Whatever our cause for intervention or bottoming out, we enter our recovery program "with our gloves on, ready to duke it out with anyone in our path". What we don't realize is that we're fighting our selves as we travel toward recovery.

In the early stages of recovery we very cautiously share our pain. When we do begin to "tell our story", we are honest and open with the story and our feelings (which are usually anger and rage). As we progress, we learn how we were reinforced to stay in our role, and we discover *our* part in the "family disease". The family disease needed us for protection, for scapegoating and as a means of pulling the family together as a unit.

In the Progression and Recovery Chart (Figure 3.2) it is noted that we hit many plateaus or relapses. At times, it appears as if we are very important in our alcoholic family because we provide a needed focus. Our job is successful because we keep the heat off everyone else in the family. By keeping the focus off others, we set a self-destructive pattern for ourselves and turn the negative attention into our form of attention and caring. We learn that our self-destructive behaviors must be fortified by building a strong wall around ourselves for protection. The bricks of our wall are made of "I don't care"; "You won't hurt me"; "I won't trust"; "Just watch me," and "I'm no good." Our bricks are cemented with tears that are never allowed to escape the bruises of abuse, the cuts and scratches of accidents and the emotional turmoil of self-destruction.

Generally, we are forced into getting help because we "need fixing". Early in our development, our parents, teachers or the court system declare, "If only we could fix this kid, this family would be normal." Early attempts are sometimes successful but many times we refuse

X

help, even though we are desperately crying for help! Quite a paradox — we throw away what we desperately desire — a chance to get out of our destruction. Sometimes our "cry for help" ends in suicide, alcohol/ drug addiction, victimization by physical or sexual abuse or a hazardous lifestyle.

Without our inner motivation, we can easily allow ourselves escape routes in our journey. The arrows to the right indicate our escape routes (or discontinuation) in our journey. If we dare to continue, our stairstep journey upward is monumental in nature. As we progress in our recovery, we start to deal with the anger that has been frozen for so very long. Because of our acceptance of inappropriate negative feelings, we become fearful of breaking our old behaviors that are so entrenched in our personality.

As we continue along our path we come upon a rule from our dysfunctional family that needs to be addressed — don't trust. Our journey demands that we trust, and trust has been totally foreign.

We discover it is not necessary to have that protective brick wall. We see that others can find positives in us, and we consciously choose to change from the "bad guy" to a self-loving individual. This self-love is very scary for us because we are afraid of feeling and getting hurt. As we begin to realize that our journey has some benefits, we make productive changes in our lives.

As Scapegoats, we have difficulty breaking the cycle of our role because we are not used to the positive of being responsible. Confusion at times leads to backslides, denial, and bricks which are temporarily put back into place. It is important that we do not give up on ourselves because we need to journey onward and deal with our immense pain. As we journey onward, we realize that our changes are making lifetime differences in our beliefs and love of self!

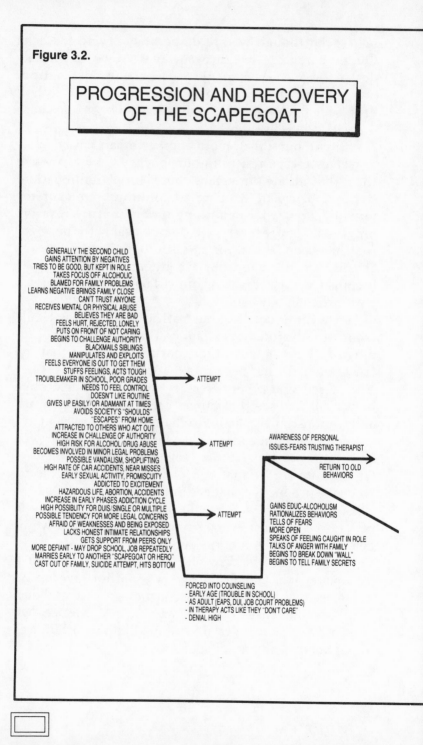

Figure 3.2.

PROGRESSION AND RECOVERY OF THE SCAPEGOAT

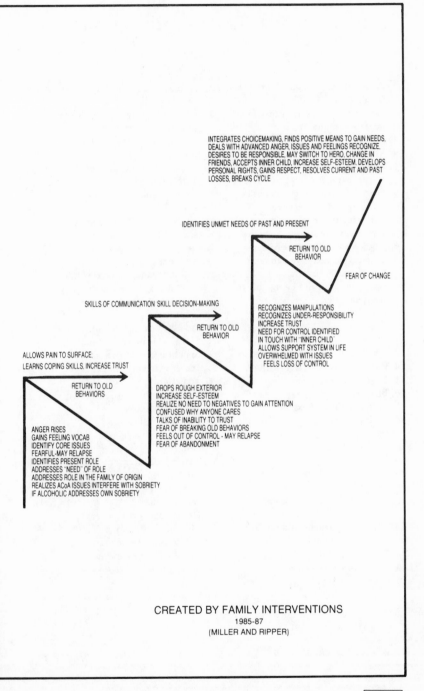

INTEGRATES CHOICEMAKING, FINDS POSITIVE MEANS TO GAIN NEEDS, DEALS WITH ADVANCED ANGER, ISSUES AND FEELINGS RECOGNIZE, DESIRES TO BE RESPONSIBLE, MAY SWITCH TO HERO, CHANGE IN FRIENDS, ACCEPTS INNER CHILD, INCREASE SELF-ESTEEM, DEVELOPS PERSONAL RIGHTS, GAINS RESPECT, RESOLVES CURRENT AND PAST LOSSES, BREAKS CYCLE

IDENTIFIES UNMET NEEDS OF PAST AND PRESENT

RETURN TO OLD BEHAVIOR

FEAR OF CHANGE

SKILLS OF COMMUNICATION SKILL DECISION-MAKING

RETURN TO OLD BEHAVIOR

RECOGNIZES MANIPULATIONS
RECOGNIZES UNDER-RESPONSIBILITY
INCREASE TRUST
NEED FOR CONTROL IDENTIFIED
IN TOUCH WITH "INNER CHILD"
ALLOWS SUPPORT SYSTEM IN LIFE
OVERWHELMED WITH ISSUES
FEELS LOSS OF CONTROL

ALLOWS PAIN TO SURFACE:
LEARNS COPING SKILLS, INCREASE TRUST

RETURN TO OLD BEHAVIORS

DROPS ROUGH EXTERIOR
INCREASE SELF-ESTEEM
REALIZE NO NEED TO NEGATIVES TO GAIN ATTENTION
CONFUSED WHY ANYONE CARES
TALKS OF INABILITY TO TRUST
FEAR OF BREAKING OLD BEHAVIORS
FEELS OUT OF CONTROL - MAY RELAPSE
FEAR OF ABANDONMENT

ANGER RISES
GAINS FEELING VOCAB
IDENTIFY CORE ISSUES
FEARFUL-MAY RELAPSE
IDENTIFIES PRESENT ROLE
ADDRESSES "NEED" OF ROLE
ADDRESSES ROLE IN THE FAMILY OF ORIGIN
REALIZES ACoA ISSUES INTERFERE WITH SOBRIETY
IF ALCOHOLIC ADDRESSES OWN SOBRIETY

CREATED BY FAMILY INTERVENTIONS
1985-87
(MILLER AND RIPPER)

STEP-BY-STEP PROGRESSION OF THE SCAPEGOAT

1. Generally the second child in the family order.
2. Learns to receive attention by negative means.
3. Acts out in the home.
4. May run away or hide.
5. Attempts to be good, but family always expects perfection.
6. Learns he/she can get attention by being bad or negative.
7. Takes focus off alcoholic; gets some sympathy from dependent.
8. Blamed for all family problems.
9. Learns that negative behavior brings family together.
10. Has feelings of not being able to trust anyone.
11. Receives mental or physical abuse.
12. Believes that he/she is bad.
13. Feels hurt, rejected, lonely.
14. Puts up a front of not caring.
15. Begins to challenge authority.
16. Blackmails siblings.
17. Manipulates and exploits.
18. Feels everyone is out to get him/her.
19. Stuffs feelings, acts tough, builds walls.
20. Denies desire to be understood.
21. Becomes a troublemaker — has poor grades, cuts classes at school.
22. Attempt by teacher/school to encourage change.
23. Needs to feel in control.
24. Doesn't like routine.
25. Gives up easily.
26. Avoids doing anything society says is good.
27. Spends time away from home whenever possible.
28. Is attracted to others who act out.
29. Increased challenging of authority.
30. Good possibility of drug/alcohol abuse.
31. Attempted intervention by school or court system.
32. Becomes involved in minor legal problems.
33. Possible vandalism, rebellion, shoplifting, car accidents.
34. Promiscuity, early sexual activity.
35. Addicted to excitement.
36. Hazardous life; addiction, abortion, accidents.
37. Increase in early stages of addiction.
38. Afraid of weaknesses and of being exposed.
39. Possible DUIs.
40. Increased possibility of legal concerns.
41. Attempted intervention by court system.
42. Lacks honest, intimate relationships.
43. Gets support from peers.
44. More defiant, may drop out of school/repeated job changes.
45. Usually marries another Scapegoat or a Responsible Child.
46. Some Scapegoats are cast out of the family, may attempt suicide.

STEP-BY-STEP RECOVERY OF THE SCAPEGOAT

1. Forced into counseling, usually at an early age (trouble in school, pregnancy, runaway) or as an adult (EAP, DUI, job problems or through court system).
2. Acts like he/she doesn't care in therapy.
3. High denial.
4. Begins to tell some "family secrets".
5. Talks of family and anger surrounding events of the past.
6. Begins to break down the "wall".
7. Tells more of family secrets and of fears.
8. Uses systematic reasoning to discount therapist's confrontations of self-destructive behaviors.
9. Awareness of being an ACoA.
10. Gains education on family disease concept.
11. Fearful of trusting therapist.
12. If alcoholic or drug dependent, needs to work with chemical dependency program — needs to be stabilized in that program before working on ACoA issues.
13. Willing to tell all family secrets.
14. Realizes that ACoA issues are interfering with sobriety or with life.
15. Investigates role in family of origin.
16. Identifies need to be "kept" as a scapegoat.
17. Identifies present role.
18. Fearful of trusting and dealing with feelings, may relapse.
19. Identifies own core issues.
20. Develops a "feeling" vocabulary.
21. Overwhelmed with anger, learns some anger-coping skills.
22. Allows the pain to surface; increases trust.
23. Fear of abandonment identified.
24. Feels out of control, may relapse.
25. Fear of breaking old patterns.
26. Talks of inability to trust.
27. Confused why anyone would care.
28. Realization that does not have to deal with negatives to gain attention, change in behaviors/takes risks.
29. Increased self-esteem, more motivation in therapy for self.
30. Learns communication skills, decision-making skills and values clarification.
31. Drops tough exterior to selected people.
32. Overwhelmed with issues; feels loss of control.
33. Starts to allow support system in life.
34. Gets in touch with "child" within.
35. Need for control identified.
36. Realizes trust may be needed.
37. Recognizes under-responsibility, manipulation.
38. Identifies unmet needs, past and present.
39. Fear of change, may relapse.
40. Recognition/identification of control issues.
41. Black/white dealings with core issues.
42. Increase in trust with others.
43. Identifies positive means to get needs met.
44. Deals with anger, advanced stage.
45. Identifies cross addictions (gambling, eating disorders, over-spending, etc.).

46. Begins to address spirituality issues.
47. Recognizes desire to be responsible.
48. Begins to address control issues.
49. Begins to plan daily life changes.
50. Identifies need for crisis/excitement.
51. Fear of sensitivity; scared of awareness, of insight into self and toward significant others.
52. Clarifies stuffed feelings.
53. Feels overwhelmed with loss of control.
54. Identifies old messages.
55. Sets boundaries.
56. Identifies how anger was vented destructively.
57. Recognition/identification of personal loss and grief issues.
58. Deals once again with childhood loss and anger.
59. May switch to "hero" if possible.
60. Learns skills of self-affirming.
61. Change in friends.
62. Identifies distorted thinking and hearing processes.
63. Learns change structure/choices.
64. Identifies advanced self-defeating behaviors.
65. Begins accepting the "child" within.
66. Acquires new interests, still a need for excitement.
67. Increased self-esteem.
68. Integrates spirituality.
69. Identifies others' rights.
70. Develops personal "bill of rights".
71. Identifies external referencing.
72. Identifies resentments.
73. Pulls from unhealthy family members and shares with other family members.
74. May be allowed new role in family of origin.
75. Gains respect of family and friends.
76. Identifies sexual or incest/abuse issues.
77. Works once again on anger issues.
78. Learns to be at ease with self.
79. Learns to be more sensitive to others.
80. Trusts selectively.
81. Permission to be responsible.
82. Accepts the "child" — integrated.
83. Integrated choicemaking.
84. Increased positive self-feelings/validates self.
85. Learns relaxation, meditation.
86. Grieves past losses, deals with current losses.
87. Decides if spouse needs to be in therapy.
88. Gets children into therapy.
89. Increased confidence in relationships, intimacy, parenting.
90. Brightened future, sets goals for future.
91. Able to identify and ask for needs to be met by family.
92. Breaks cycle.

E

THERAPEUTIC ISSUES

Because of our strong defenses, we are typically difficult clients for many therapists. Perhaps that's why so many therapists quit on us in therapy. Of course the rejection and surrendering of the therapist allows us to build our bricks higher and higher for fortification. We truly need love and understanding which can only develop with time and support. Once we see that our journey is worth the fight, we will not let our recovery be halted — we will fight with our very life for our journey home!

Therapists have to be comfortable with our anger and rage which needs to be vented. Therapists must realize the anger that is being constantly vented is not directed at them, but is the anger that has been stored internally for years.

We need to learn how to constructively use our anger in a positive manner, as well as learn how to use coping mechanisms to deal successfully with our feelings. Because we have spent our lifetime denying our feelings, we need psychoeducational training in "feelings" identification. Another basic skill that must be addressed is responsible decision-making and values clarification. Choicemaking is an essential part of our recovery, because we need extensive work with the identification of our needs. Once we become aware of our needs, we must then learn the healthy means by which we can attain those needs.

Due to our inconsistent unpredictable lives, it is imperative that our therapists be consistent. If our therapists are repeatedly late or cancel appointments, we will see such actions as similar to those of all the others who just don't care! Another issue that is important in our recovery is having an environment where we can feel love, caring and support. This environment can produce a setting where it is safe to explore our inner self.

As we journey along our path, we need constantly to be made aware of the positives and/or payoffs of our new behavior. Without that constant verification of our progress, we will quickly revert back to our old self-destructive behaviors. Our recovery increases our self-respect and self-esteem.

The Cowardly Lion
(The Lost Child)

The Cowardly Lion blends into the camouflaged lush backdrop of the forest. His being enmeshes with the greens and browns and he is unnoticed by the passing intruders. Being a lion, however, he realizes his role mandates some contrived and forced behaviors — he must at least appear courageous, brave and fearless. As the Cowardly Lion leaps from his hiding place, he attempts to portray his role with authenticity. The inner struggle of portraying something he is not creates great confusion, shame, guilt and fear within.

As Lost Children we feel this enmeshment with our environment. In fact, it is our mainstay and fortification of our survival. By enmeshing with the environment, we are lost in the lush greenery of the forest. That greenery becomes an escape from intruders and chaos. It becomes a place of safety and security. The greenery may consist of an escape in artistic drawings, reading, imaginary friends, fantasies or the humanization of inanimate objects.

But the greenery does not always cover up the feelings that constantly emerge. The role we portray in life doesn't mask the inner pain — it masks only the external shell. For example, externally the Cowardly Lion appears brave and courageous (his role), but internally he is engulfed with fears and insecurities.

Many of us use other mechanisms to escape from the role and from reality. Methods used may include some of the following: overeating, overspending, sexual addictions or substance abuse. All are vehicles used to mask emerging feelings.

Common Characteristics of the Lost Child

- We are usually the third child in the family birth order.
- We feel like loners, outsiders.

R

- We find comfort in privacy.
- We have underdeveloped communication skills.
- We get our needs filled out of the "mind".
- We are likely to have an eating disorder, specifically bulimia.
- We have had little experience with human closeness.
- We doubt our sexual normalcy.
- We see our sexual identity as a concern.
- We have feelings of loneliness, worthlessness.
- We have a high rate of allergies, asthma.
- We feel an emotional emptiness.
- We have a lot of pride in materialism (car, pets, stereo, etc.).
- We often abuse drugs and/or alcohol.
- We maintain a low profile and "fade into the woodwork".
- We have a high creativity level, especially in writing, art, philosophy.
- We have a high rate of depression, anxiety and panic disorders.
- We have a good chance of success in treatment.
- We take slow, deliberate steps in recovery.

The role of the Lost Child only allows minimal contact with people. Therefore, we do not receive any indications of our positives from those around us. As Lost Children we see ourselves as "in the way" and at times we even question our right to live. This belief manifests itself in several ways.

1. The family reinforces the role.
2. A protection device is commonly used.
3. There is a fantasy world versus reality.
4. Total mistrust of self exists.

A. Family's Reinforcement of the Role

As Lost Children we don't see a place within the family for ourselves and conclude that the best way to help is by doing nothing. The family reinforces this belief with statements such as, "I never have problems with her"; "I'm so glad you stay out of the way"; "She always keeps her mouth shut and does what she is told" or "He's so good, I don't even know he's around."

Through these messages that we receive from significant others, we come to truly believe that we are helping our families by not being a part of our family. We compound these messages by telling ourselves that this also holds true outside the family. For example, in school we stayed removed from the teacher because we saw the teacher as an authority figure, like our parents. We assumed that if our parents wanted us to act this way, then it would follow that our teachers wanted us to act in the same manner.

Visualize a classroom in which you were a member, either as a student or as a teacher. Now look around the room. Which names do you recall easily and which names are you having difficulty remembering? There might even be a child in that class that you would never recall unless someone happened to mention his/her name. Those children are the Lost Children.

We also receive messages from our siblings that are similar to those received from our parents. The general messages are "Go away, you are just in the way"; "Don't pay any attention to her, she doesn't know what's going on"; "Oh, how long have you been here?" or the worst thing that can happen — nobody recognizes our presence at all!

We translate these into messages such as, "I am in the way" and "My opinion is meaningless." Not only are our opinions meaningless, but they wouldn't count even if we gave them. Because we believe that our opinions and behaviors are worthless and meaningless, then *we* are worthless. We become engulfed in shame over our very existence. From these messages come more descriptive, destructive messages and ways of behaving.

B. Protection Device

As Lost Children we live in terror. The terror comes from a feeling that something awful will happen to the entire family or that Mom or Dad will abandon us (emotionally or physically.) We fear that we will be left alone, helpless and hopeless. To avoid these feelings, we choose one of two ways of reacting: (1) we believe that what we don't see won't hurt us, or (2) we continuously decide not to leave the home because something awful might happen while we are gone. When something looks threatening to us, we hide in a safe place either with a view of the situation or totally removed from the situation. If we are at home, we either retreat to our room or around the corner with the wall as our shield. Whatever place we chose, it is a place that we perceive as safe. If our safe place isn't close, we retreat into our imaginations and fantasies.

C. Fantasy World Versus Reality

Everyone has fantasies. These fantasies are normal and healthy because they can allow us a *temporary release* from stress. As Lost Children we live in a fantasy world that we have created for ourselves. This distorted thinking makes it very difficult for us to distinguish between what our positives actually are and what we wish they would be. Not only can we not distinguish our positives, but we are unable to distinguish the real world from our fantasy world. This can leave *us* very confused as well as *those around us.* Because of the isolation we have chosen, we have escaped from events physically and emotionally. This has caused us to have little knowledge of what occurs during our absences. Because of our escapes, we have a low reality base from which to work.

D. Total Mistrust of Self

As a result of the previous three factors, we do not trust any of our feelings, thoughts or decisions. We see ourselves as unable to believe anything that happens to us. When we become frightened, or a situation appears to be too difficult to handle, we retreat into a fantasy world.

As a result of our isolation, Lost Children are self-taught and have strengths that lie in the behaviors that are acted on individually or have been self-taught.

THE POSITIVE SIDE OF THE LOST CHILD

The Wizard methodically turns to the Lion and states that he is a victim of unorganized, distorted thinking. The Wizard retorts, "You are under the unfortunate delusion that you have no courage, merely because you run from danger. You are confusing courage with wisdom." The Wizard continues his proclamation as he gives the triumphant hero an enormous, triple-cross medal. The Wizard describes his bravery and valor and includes him in the infamous "Legion of Courage".

As Lost Children we quietly nurture our inner fears, just as the Cowardly Lion nurtured his fear of not performing appropriately as King of the Jungle. Ironically, the courage was always a part of the Lion, just as the ability to escape from our personal isolation was always a part of us. The power to be whatever we desire to be is truly attainable for those of us who take the risk to address personal recovery.

Before you read on, write down the positives that have been developed and learned as a result of this role. It doesn't matter if this is your role or not. Look at the strengths of the role. (Please do not feel limited by the numbering.)

1 _____ 2 _____

3 _____ 4 _____

5 _____ 6 _____

7 _____ 8 _____

9 _____ 10 _____

11 _____ 12 _____

13 _____ 14 _____

15 _____ 16 _____

17 _____ 18 _____

19 _____ 20 _____

SOME POSITIVES FOR THE LOST CHILD

THE LOST CHILD . . .

can work independently
is self-reliant
is loyal
enjoys time alone
can show emotions
is punctual
is flexible
is compassionate
has a good imagination
is courteous
appreciates aesthetics
is trustworthy
is methodical
is empathetic
is very appreciative
is inventive, artistic
has patience
makes steady progress in
   therapy

completes projects
is dependable
doesn't set unrealistic
   expectations
cares about others
is sensitive
has high morals
comfortable to be with
is a good listener
is creative
pays attention to detail
is logical
takes care of others'
   possessions
appreciates friends
accepts own pace
is a fast learner
makes a good worker
can delay gratification

Lost Children generally choose careers that allow us to use our assets, such as writers, painters, accountants, one-person office workers, editors, etc. These professions reduce the frustration and fear that occurs when working with the public or with a large number of coworkers. We like jobs which require little supervision and that give us the independence to regulate our own timetable. A Lost Child stays with a job for long periods of time because it is a place of safety and is non-threatening. This is due to having accumulated knowledge and expertise in the job and the responsibilities attached to the job. This increased security diminishes the risk of being criticized for our mistakes.

Place within this medal of courage the positives that you possess from this role. Include with an asterisk (*) the characteristics you desire to integrate into your journey.

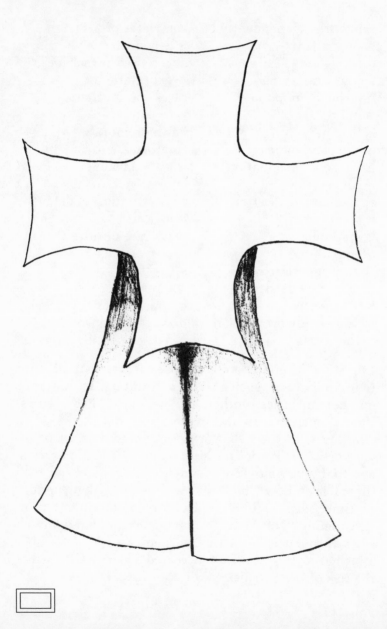

The Progression and Recovery of the Lost Child

The foursome stand at the palace gates awaiting the meeting with the Magnificent Oz, who will hopefully grant their wishes. The Cowardly Lion dreams of gaining what he is missing — courage. Without the courage he desires, he will be ignored by the other members of the forest. Without that courage, he will not be unique or special. Without that courage, he fears, he will not be King of the Forest!

The progression of the role of the Lost Child is much different from any of the other family roles. Our siblings gradually progress into their roles while our progression is almost like jumping off a cliff. The first attention we received after birth was the slap on the rear, and after that, it feels as if we are taken for granted and ignored for the rest of our lives. Because the Lost Child is usually third in the birth order, nothing we did in infancy was unique. Everything had already been done by our older siblings (either developing faster or slower than the "norm"), so we just fade into the family.

From the beginning we use the process of escapism. Due to our early recognition of our lack of purpose within the family, we fade into the background and isolate ourselves. It needs to be noted that we choose to continue our isolation by keeping ourselves removed from the family and not showing others our special qualities. Due to this choice, we are forced either to be self-taught or not to learn what we need. The need for personal satisfaction is fulfilled through books, day-dreams, food, imaginary friends and/or family or our personal inner creativity. Our development is often repressed because we are self-taught — whether that be socially, physically or emotionally. As Lost Children we seem to slip through the cracks, being passed by, neglected to be noticed (almost as though we didn't exist) and isolated from others.

Figure 3.3.

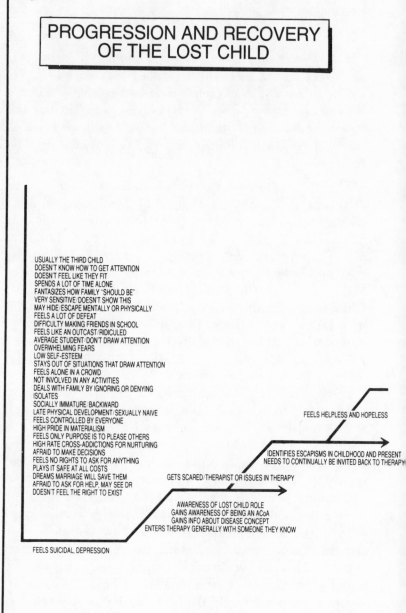

PROGRESSION AND RECOVERY OF THE LOST CHILD

USUALLY THE THIRD CHILD
DOESN'T KNOW HOW TO GET ATTENTION
DOESN'T FEEL LIKE THEY FIT
SPENDS A LOT OF TIME ALONE
FANTASIZES HOW FAMILY "SHOULD BE"
VERY SENSITIVE/DOESN'T SHOW THIS
MAY HIDE/ESCAPE MENTALLY OR PHYSICALLY
FEELS A LOT OF DEFEAT
DIFFICULTY MAKING FRIENDS IN SCHOOL
FEELS LIKE AN OUTCAST/RIDICULED
AVERAGE STUDENT/DON'T DRAW ATTENTION
OVERWHELMING FEARS
LOW SELF-ESTEEM
STAYS OUT OF SITUATIONS THAT DRAW ATTENTION
FEELS ALONE IN A CROWD
NOT INVOLVED IN ANY ACTIVITIES
DEALS WITH FAMILY BY IGNORING OR DENYING
ISOLATES
SOCIALLY IMMATURE/BACKWARD
LATE PHYSICAL DEVELOPMENT/SEXUALLY NAIVE
FEELS CONTROLLED BY EVERYONE
HIGH PRIDE IN MATERIALISM
FEELS ONLY PURPOSE IS TO PLEASE OTHERS
HIGH RATE CROSS-ADDICTIONS FOR NURTURING
AFRAID TO MAKE DECISIONS
FEELS NO RIGHTS TO ASK FOR ANYTHING
PLAYS IT SAFE AT ALL COSTS
DREAMS MARRIAGE WILL SAVE THEM
AFRAID TO ASK FOR HELP, MAY SEE DR
DOESN'T FEEL THE RIGHT TO EXIST

FEELS HELPLESS AND HOPELESS

IDENTIFIES ESCAPISMS IN CHILDHOOD AND PRESENT
NEEDS TO CONTINUALLY BE INVITED BACK TO THERAPY

GETS SCARED/THERAPIST OR ISSUES IN THERAPY

AWARENESS OF LOST CHILD ROLE
GAINS AWARENESS OF BEING AN ACoA
GAINS INFO ABOUT DISEASE CONCEPT
ENTERS THERAPY GENERALLY WITH SOMEONE THEY KNOW

FEELS SUICIDAL, DEPRESSION

L

BEGINS TO TAKE RESPONSIBILITY FOR LIFE, ALLOWS OTHERS TO "KNOW THEM", TAKES SMALL RISKS, DEALS WITH ANGER, ACCEPTS CHILD WITHIN, DEALS WITH FEARS OF ABANDONMENT, DEALS WITH ANGER & RESENTMENTS, IDENTIFIES AND ADDRESSES NEEDS NOT MET, DEALS WITH INTIMACY AND PARENTING CONCERNS, LEARNS TO HAVE FUN, INCREASES SELF-WORTH, SELF-ESTEEM RISES, DEVELOPS FAMILY GOALS, DEALS GRIEF ISSUES, BREAKS THE CYCLE

FEAR OF CHANGE

RECOGNIZES SELF-DEFEATING BEHAVIORS
REALIZES RIGHT TO BE ANGRY
RECOGNIZES CONTROL ISSUES

FEAR OF TAKING RESPONSIBILITY FOR SELF

SEES CHILDHOOD MORE REALISTICALLY
LEARNS TO SAY "NO"
DEALS WITH PEOPLE-PLEASING

OVERWHELMED/FEELS LOSS OF CONTROL

TALKS OF MORE SECRETS
DEALS WITH MIND READING AND SCANNING

TELLS THERAPIST "SECRETS-FEARFUL OF ABANDONMENT"

GETS IN TOUCH WITH "INNER CHILD"
DEVELOPS A FEELING VOCABULARY
DEVELOPS COMMUNICATION SKILLS

CREATED BY FAMILY INTERVENTIONS
1985-87
(MILLER AND RIPPER)

STEP-BY-STEP PROGRESSION OF THE LOST CHILD

1. Usually third child in family order.
2. Doesn't know how to get attention.
3. Doesn't feel like he/she fits into the family.
4. Spends a lot of time alone.
5. High rate of allergies, asthma, accidents.
6. Fantasizes about the way family and self "should" be.
7. Very sensitive but doesn't show it.
8. May hide under the bed, in the attic, etc. during stressful situations.
9. Feels a lot of defeat.
10. Has difficulty making friends in school.
11. Feels like an outcast — peers ridicule him/her.
12. Average student.
13. Overwhelming fears/feelings stuffed.
14. Very low self-esteem.
15. Stays out of situations that would draw attention to self.
16. Feels alone in a crowd.
17. Fears abandonment.
18. Not involved in any school activities.
19. Deals with family problems by ignoring or denying them.
20. When wanting to be with other children, hangs around siblings and their friends.
21. Socially immature/backwards.
22. Late physical development.
23. Sexually naive.
24. Feels controlled by everyone.
25. Attempts to gain self-control by use of food, numbing, escaping, etc.
26. Willing to do anything for friendship.
27. High pride in materialism.
28. Neglects own needs.
29. Cries alone — feels a lot of hurt and pain, but keeps to self.
30. Dreams of relationships with opposite sex.
31. May be used sexually by opposite sex due to wanting to be accepted.
32. Feels his/her only purpose is to please others.
33. Does things for family but is never recognized.
34. High level of denial about personal situation and family situation.
35. Jealous/envious of siblings.
36. Blends into the woodwork.
37. Has difficulty knowing self.
38. Wants out of the home.
39. May get pregnant to leave home.
40. Dreams of marrying a Responsible Child, but usually marries another Lost Child.
41. Becomes unhealthily attached to children — over protective — feels children are the only people who truly love him/her.
42. Afraid to make decisions.
43. Never feels the right to ask for anything.
44. Afraid to take any risks — plays it safe at all costs.
45. High level of depression.
46. Afraid to ask for help — may seek a doctor but identify problems through physical symptoms.
47. May develop phobias.
48. May develop cross-addictions such as eating disorders, drug use, over-spending, etc.
49. Doesn't feel the right to exist.
50. Suicide attempts — "cries for help".
51. Either suicide by mistake or intention of suicide.

STEP-BY-STEP RECOVERY OF THE LOST CHILD

1. Feels desperate to change life.
2. Enters therapy, but generally with someone they know or because of being overwhelmed by feelings of loneliness and undefined fears.
3. Gains awareness of being an ACoA.
4. Awareness of lost child role.
5. Gets education on family disease, how alcoholism affected their life pattern.
6. Gets scared of therapist and/or therapy and leaves or becomes somewhat dependent on therapist.
7. Needs to be continually invited back to therapy.
8. Starts to identify escapism in childhood.
9. Starts to identify escapism in present life.
10. Feels hopeless and helpless.
11. Learns to open up more in therapy/selective trusting.
12. Joins group with recognition of others who have the same undefined fear.
13. Identifies other ACoA core issues.
14. Develops some communication skills.
15. Develops a "feeling" vocabulary.
16. High concern that they cannot recall events from their childhood.
17. Gets in touch with inner "child".
18. Cautiously uses feelings in therapy — opens up more to therapist.
19. Tells therapist "secrets" in present life (overeating, purging, binging, chemical use).
20. Fearful of therapist's view of self.
21. Identifies mind-reading patterns in therapy.
22. Identifies mind-reading patterns of childhood.
23. Deals minimally with secrets of present.
24. Overwhelmed with issues, feels loss of control.
25. Unsure of making decisions or making change.
26. Speaks of people pleasing in past and present.
27. Starts to recognize unmet needs.
28. Fear of being rejected; relapse possible.
29. Recognition/identification of under- or over-responsibility.
30. Learns to say "no" in small doses.
31. Learns decision-making and values clarification.
32. Fear of taking responsibility for self.
33. Recognizes methods of control in self.
34. Learns of "secrets" and childhood loss, sees childhood more realistically.
35. Develops fear of abandonment by therapist/clarifies feelings of abandonment.
36. Fearful of loss of known behaviors — feels a void.
37. Fearful of feelings.
38. Recognizes control issues/starts to let go selectively.
39. Realizes right to be angry.
40. Fear of anger, insight in self and anger toward family members.
41. Recognizes self-defeating behaviors/addresses cross-addictions.
42. Fear of change, may relapse.

I

43. Begins to take responsibility for own life to small degree, begins to allow people to know them.
44. Progress good and steady, person now does feel more comfortable with progress.
45. Deals with stuffed feelings/begins to pinpoint feelings with accuracy.
46. Begins to take calculated risks.
47. Increased <u>real</u> talking.
48. Starts to learn who to trust.
49. Learns to accept some compliments, rewards.
50. Fearful of own feelings.
51. Identifies need to not be alone.
52. Fear of loss of control, need to escape.
53. Recognizes and identifies personal anger issues.
54. Scared to address anger, need to escape.
55. Identifies old "defeating messages".
56. Fear of change.
57. Recognizes and identifies personal loss and grief issues.
58. Identifies distorted thinking and hearing, fantasies and continued mind-reading.
59. Decreased need for approval.
60. Advanced work on self-defeating behaviors.
61. Learns process of change structure and boundaries clarification.
62. Begins to break dependency with therapist.
63. Begins accepting "child within".
64. Sets own personal "bill of rights".
65. Identifies external referencing.
66. Identifies compulsive loving.
67. Grieves past abandonment/faces fear, anger and hurt.
68. Begins to identify friends who "use".
69. Starts to find healthy friends, minimizes unhealthy friendships.
70. Clarifies needs not met in past/present.
71. Clarifies resentments cautiously. Fearful of dealing with resentments.
72. Advanced anger work.
73. Pulls from unhealthy family and/or begins to talk to family members about family secrets in home of origin.
74. Begins taking responsibility for self.
75. Learns to ask and gain needs attainment.
76. Allows others to know them.
77. Trusts appropriately.
78. Identifies sexual or incest/abuse issues.
79. Learns relaxation/meditation.
80. Accepts the "child" within.
81. Integrates spirituality.
82. Deals with relationships, intimacy and parenting issues.
83. Able to identify personal needs <u>and</u> ask for needs to be met by family and others.
84. Family ties become stronger.
85. Advanced work with abandonment and resentment.
86. Learns to have fun with others.
87. Grieves past losses.
88. Gives self-permission to be part of a group.
89. Expresses positive "self" feelings.
90. Increased self-worth, self-esteem.
91. Gives self permission to be happy and sets personal future goals.
92. Develops family goals.
93. Breaks cycle.

Many times our escapism finds us trying to personally meet our unmet childhood needs. We are unaware of this because we are unaware of the needs that exist within us. Because of our needs, we learn some powerful survival skills that can be self destructive to our progression. Many of us develop into bulimics, anorexics (rarely) or phobics. Sexual issues are of great concern to us, but we are too frightened to pursue the issue. This fear can result from isolation, incest in childhood or distorted facts about sexuality. We learned little about sexuality because our fear kept us from the facts and reality.

In some cases, our prolonged pain and depression leads to a "bottoming out" which brings us helplessly searching for help. At this point we find a caretaker who may assist in the journey into recovery. At our crisis we become desperate to gain help because we feel that we are going crazy and the old (self-destructive) patterns no longer seem to work. Unfortunately, some of us are "too lost" to reach out for help and therefore fall deeper into depression.

Looking at the Progression and Recovery Charts (Figure 3.3), we see that our recovery is slow and steady. Many "secrets" must be uncovered from the past. As we learn of our role's progression, we come in contact with a childhood that was blackened out or forgotten. We discover that we numbed ourselves, escaped, or physically took ourselves away from the trauma of our homes of origin. We now must discover the realities and facts of our childhood. As we go onward in our recovery, we begin to seek out answers about our pasts. We begin to explore the cycles of escape and the means of survival used, as well as our self-destructive behaviors.

We may become fearful of the feelings and knowledge that arise during therapy and once again desire an escape. The short stair-steps illustrate the small, steady progress we make, as well as the constant fears of going forward. Fear may lead to relapse or discontinuation of the recovery journey. This is indicated by the flat portion of the chart and the arrows pointing to the right. We often regress and enter denial once again, but, hopefully, we will return to address our fears and move onward.

THERAPEUTIC ISSUES

Talking about the "secrets" is quite scary for us. We must constantly be reinvited into therapy because we are unsure about whether or not we have over-stayed our welcome during the session. Because of our mistrust of others, we have major abandonment issues that must be addressed in the recovery process.

As Lost Children we must be given much support and patience as we rediscover our pasts. We need constant encouragement and help to set small goals so that we may push onward. Therapy must be loving and caring with little confrontation. Confrontation scares us! The therapist must be gentle with us along the way. Pushing us too hard gives us an excuse to escape into fantasies or causes us to "numb out". It is helpful if we are given small tasks that will teach us risk-taking and the general comfort of being success-oriented. We need to gain confidence in ourselves.

Facing the reality of what occurred in our past, as well as what may occur in therapy, is taking a big risk. It helps to know where we are going — this eases our fears. We no longer are afraid of being afraid.

Our "escaping" did not allow development of daily living skills. Our journey needs to deal with life's stresses and coping skills, choicemaking, values clarification, needs identification, feelings identification and management skills that we did not learn as children.

It is also essential that the therapist address our cross-addictions (overspending, eating disorders, drug or alcohol abuse, etc.) and make referrals to other thera-

Z

pists if needed. Many of us have eating disorders that require specialized treatment modalities.

Sharon Wegscheider-Cruse describes our recovery process as slow, but generally we have a high success rate. Our journey into the unknown is a change that makes a lifetime difference.

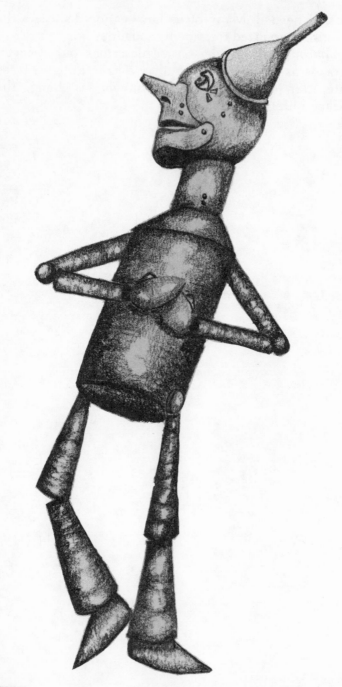

The Tin Man (The Mascot)

As Dorothy and the Scarecrow continue their journey on the Yellow Brick Road, they discover the immobilized Tin Man, helplessly rusted in the apple orchard. The duo rescues the Tin Man from his imprisonment. Free at last, the Tin Man is elated about his ability to move once again. Dorothy notes that the Tin Man is now "perfect" after the oiling of his rusted locked joints. The Tin Man is quick to tell them of his deficiency — the Woodsman forgot to give him a HEART! As he describes his despair, he sings for the onlookers, "If I only had a heart . . ."

The Tin Man describes feeling incomplete and inadequate. Without a vital organ, he feels hollow and without an inner guiding force. Deficient of the "guiding system", he believes that he must change and alter himself to adapt to others. He becomes unsure and fearful of the feelings, wants and needs emerging inside himself.

The Mascot in a dysfunctional family feels the need to change and adapt to others. Mascots are typically overly sensitive individuals who desperately want to be loved. We typically do not realize, just as the Tin Man, that we *do* have a heart! Our wounded heart keeps us locked in our role of adapting and changing for others. Mascots become hypervigilant, scanning the environment for clues on how to alter our behavior. The behavior exhibited is that of altering oneself to become what others desire. We hope that by altering our true selves we will achieve the love that we desire.

Mascots are mandated by feelings (the heart) which we desperately wish we could control. Personal control means not feeling so crazy; not feeling so unsure of who we are; not feeling shame about concealing the family secrets; not feeling like we are trapped in the "baby" role and not feeling as though we must always entertain and pacify others. Most importantly, gaining personal

A

control might be the prerequisite for allowing personal exploration and normalcy.

Common Characteristics of the Mascot

- We are usually the last child (baby) of the family.
- We are usually the "class clown" in school.
- We have had vital information withheld from us for fear that we can't "handle it" or need protection.
- We have been over-protected.
- We contribute to the family by pleasing the family and comic relief.
- We feel like chameleons.
- We refuse to take things seriously, at times, for an escape.
- We are not thought of seriously.
- We are usually smaller in size that our siblings.
- We sometimes feel like we are going crazy.
- We may have many compulsive or annoying behaviors.
- We have difficulty with commitment in relationships.
- We have a high degree of Ritalin use at school age.
- We harbor massive feelings of fear.
- We hide behind our "clown face" and others find it difficult to really know us.
- We feel inadequate, unimportant, manipulated.
- We have low self-worth.
- We may remain a "child" forever.
- We have trouble accepting others' feelings.
- We have difficulty expressing our feelings.
- We have a high incidence of substance abuse.
- We have a fear of insanity, fear of suicidal tendencies.
- We are extremely sensitive.
- We feel that we are taking on all the family feelings (pain).

The Mascot's siblings are usually very jealous of us because our role receives many payoffs. However, as Mascots our biggest problem is that others do not take us seriously. Because others treat us like babies or don't take us seriously, we tend to doubt ourselves and our worth. As Mascots we can list our positives easier than our siblings can. On the other hand, we have a harder time believing the truth in these positives.

Because of our role, we have very likeable personalities. We are the type of person that others want to be around when they are feeling down. We can always make people laugh by cracking a joke, acting like a clown to get a whole crowd happy or simply performing our own special "magic" to bring a smile to the faces of our audience. "Fun" is our middle name. We know how to have a good time and can make it contagious. The Enabler and the Responsible Child see us as totally irresponsible, but secretly they admire us for our enjoyment of life.

The Mascot has a good sense of timing and knows when to step in to lighten things up. We can ease tension with our timing and spontaneity. Unfortunately, we sometimes get carried away and push the humor too far.

Our humor is usually based on our own experiences, which makes us excellent performers. We watch carefully to see which "act" will work with each particular audience. Our humor comes from paying attention to details and watching (hypervigilance) others' behaviors, idiosyncrasies, mannerisms, and speech patterns. These patterns are magnified and related in a comical style.

Most people don't know that we are extremely sensitive souls who truly want to love! We believe that our performance will earn the applause of love and caring. We find ourselves desperately trying to be anything others want us to be in order to feel good inside. Outsiders never see the hollowness we feel. We conceal this pain with humor and people-pleasing. Because of our ability to blend with so many people, we can usually be easily spotted in a crowd. It's easy to identify Mascots because we are usually in the middle, entertaining those around us. This role is manifested by four factors:

1. There is protection by the family.
2. We fulfill the family's need for humor.
3. We are never taken seriously.
4. Distrust of facts.

A. Protection By The Family

Because we are usually the youngest, the family believes we need to be protected from unpleasant truths. They protect us in several ways: (1) everyone stops talking when we enter the room; (2) the family distorts or lessens the facts of an unpleasant situation; (3) the family diverts our attention from the situation or (4) they bluntly tell us that we don't need to know. The family thinks that because we are "the baby of the family", we will never grow up and we will always think and act like a child. Unfortunately, we take our family very seriously.

B. Family's Need For Humor

The Mascot is usually the youngest child, which means that many times the family alcoholic has progressed into the late stages of alcoholism during the Mascot's early childhood. Because of the high stress in the family, a relief from the pressure is needed. This relief is fulfilled by the family Mascot. In order to reduce, divert or distract the family from the stress, the family turns to us to make them laugh and break the tension. We are the ones who enable the family or individual to take a temporary vacation, which is essential for everyone.

T

C. Never Taken Seriously

As Mascots we are seen as not having a care in the world and always having smiles on our faces. The family believes that because it hides family problems from us, we are unaware of the situation. Due to these two beliefs, the family thinks that we can not be hurting because we are shielded from pain. Thus when we attempt to share our thoughts or feelings, we are pushed aside and not taken seriously. We are trapped within our pain knowing the problems exist but we are isolated by our role.

D. Distrust Of Facts

Everyone in the family is a master of distortion. Reality can be effectively altered to become a family illusion. Because the reality distortions are so frequent, we do not develop an ability to distinguish fact from fiction. We feel as though we are going crazy at times due to the conflicting stories. To avoid the confusion, we choose to do one of three things: (1) forget everything we hear and pretend it has not happened; (2) make light of everything and turn it into the family joke or (3) become our own private investigator.

Being a private investigator is difficult because we usually have to go out of the family for information that we can believe is accurate. This is dangerous because going outside the family means breaking one of the family rules — "don't talk about it". This can become a really push-pull conflict. We want to know, but it is very difficult to break a very important, unspoken rule. This stress leads to exhaustion and many of us therefore drop being the private investigator.

The Positive Side of The Mascot

The Wizard turns to the clanking Tin Man, who is hoping for his long-awaited heart. The Wizard informs the Tin Man that he is quite lucky not to be trapped by the feelings of pain and sensitivity that others experience. Despite the Wizard's warnings, the Tin Man still desperately wants his heart. The Wizard continues his oration and gives the awaiting Tin Man a huge heart-shaped watch that actually ticks like a real beating heart. He concludes his speech with the ominous statement, "Remember, my sentimental friend, a heart isn't judged by how much you love, but by how much you are loved by others."

The family Mascot is just as sensitive and sentimental as our hero, the Tin Man. As Mascots, we typically wear our hearts on our sleeve and will do anything for those we love, including altering our own personality. The heart can be a positive attribute if the positive is turned inward. As Mascots we have a large reservoir of love that we can give to ourselves. This love allows us to find ourselves and accept who and what we truly are inside. We need to give ourselves permission to do this.

The Wizard's statement about love was misstated — love is *not* measured by how much others love you, but by how much you can love yourself. That love is the greatest love of all.

Before you read on, write down the positives that have been developed and learned as a result of this role. It doesn't matter if this is your role or not. Look at the strengths of the role. (Please do not feel limited by the numbering.)

1 _____   3 _____

2 _____   4 _____

THE POSITIVE LIST FOR THE MASCOT IS AS FOLLOWS

THE MASCOT . . .

is spontaneous
is fun to work with
shares responsibilities
lightens and eases tension
attracts friends
is humorous
is compassionate
has a positive approach
  (attitudes)
will take co-leadership
  role
knows how to have and
  create fun
is very adaptable
can identify people who
  need humor
has a good sense of timing
is sensitive
is inventive
is imaginative
has quick responses
is protective of friends
is a good listener
is attuned to people

has self-motivation
is adventurous
is loyal
pays attention to details
  about others and their
  mannerisms
is a good manager
is caring, empathetic
is creative
blends with many
  different people
simulates people around
  them
is a high achiever
is very energetic
is self-motivating
has a diverse personality
takes risks
love challenges
is flexible
is a good negotiator
is a quick thinker
is good in a crisis
is excitement-oriented

The Mascot's nature is to be around people. Due to this attribute, we assume jobs that allow us to use these characteristics, such as those of acting, public relations, broadcasting, radio announcing, comedy, advertising, etc.

I

Place within this ticking heart the positives that you possess from this role. Include with an asterisk (*) the characteristics you desire to integrate into your journey.

The Progression and Recovery of The Mascot

Silence fills the air in the apple orchard. The rusty, creaky Tin Man stands erect, unable to move. The Tin Man is dependent on someone else to end his imprisonment. The key to his freedom is just out of his reach. Carelessly, the Tin Man neglected to place the oil can within his grasp — his shame keeps him rusty and immobile for over a year. The trapped Tin Man is imprisoned by his own protective armor!

Discovering the fact that there is a need for change is probably most difficult for those of us who are Mascots. The payoffs for our role are numerous and quite satisfying. Our payoffs include attention, protection, humor, friendships and excitement. On the other hand, our pain is hidden by the "tears of a clown" masquerade. This cover-up camouflages thoughts of insanity, confusion in who we are, the shame of not being taken seriously, our inner isolation, feelings of inadequacy, unimportance and the anger of feeling used by others.

Our early progression (Progression and Recovery Chart, Figure 3.4) is marked by many attempts by others to discontinue our camouflaging role. Teachers are calling home to talk to our parents about behavior that is disruptive, the principal talks to us about the constant showing off, the clergy tells us we must be mature and grow up and our family tells us to stop being so overly sensitive about everything! Attempts by others generally fail. It is hard for us to take off the mask of the clown that is our means of survival. Under the clown mask, we are sensitive and caring and in immense pain. Our pain is so great that we are fearful of a possible explosion of rage. To protect ourselves from this catastrophe, we continue the comic relief at our own expense. Our inner turmoil is often deadened by use of alcohol or other drugs.

Many of us never seem to grow up — it's almost as if we are the *real* Peter Pan! To hide the pain, we continue to make others laugh while we are feeling devastated by our own suicidal tendencies. We live in constant fear of the person who is hiding inside. Many of us "hit bottom" and enter recovery with the presenting concern of feeling like we are going crazy.

As we begin our recovery (See Progression and Recovery Chart, Figure 3.4), many of us minimize the effects of our alcoholic home. Because of the payoffs of our role, we discontinue our journey and continue along the old, self-destructive path (illustrated by the arrow along the bottom, to the right). Others of us learn the facts and characteristics of our dysfunctional role and decide we were the fortunate ones who were not affected in any way (indicated by the second arrow along the bottom). Fortunately, some of us courageously struggle along our path to recovery.

As we proceed, our problems are generally minimized because "Hey, it's no big deal . . . chuckle . . . chuckle . . ." We talk of the pain, giggling and joking compulsively throughout, minimizing our shame.

Recovery is slow, but the journey allows us a means of openly dealing with the stuffed feelings and grief. We now have an average for productive self-acceptance. Relapses along the way are quite frequent, as we are fearful of new changes. If we choose to deal with our fears, we can break through our armor to find our inner selves.

THERAPEUTIC ISSUES

We need a therapist who is able to see beneath our masks and not buy into the "cuteness" that we use to hide the issues. Many of us drop out of therapy, using the excuse that we prefer life as a clown. If therapy is continued, we become angry with the issues of never being taken seriously. We express our resentments about everyone treating us like the "little baby" who can't handle any of the family concerns. We are sure, in fact, that we knew the secrets and were always working hard to fix the problems. Didn't anyone else see what we were doing? We fight the inner turmoil and craziness that we feel so deeply inside.

Therapists must be able to work through our distorted thinking process and show us the payoffs for changes. Great progress can be made if the therapist taps into our sensitivity and need for dealing with our feelings at a deep level. We learn through therapy to say "no", as well as decision-making techniques that deal with OUR issues, not everyone else's. Emphasis must be placed on our needs, and our dedication to find the true self within! Our feelings become a part of us that we no longer fear as we learn to set personal boundaries. Most importantly, we learn to develop a "bill of rights" for ourselves.

As we travel on, we need to learn about healthy means to deal with feelings and how to have healthy relationships with others without using manipulation. As recovery progresses, we must learn to *balance* responsibility, fun and relaxation. Along the path we find our self and truly learn to love what we find inside.

Figure 3.4.

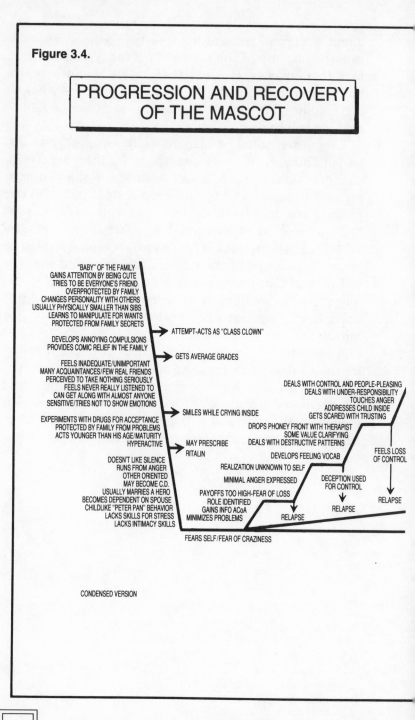

PROGRESSION AND RECOVERY
OF THE MASCOT

"BABY" OF THE FAMILY
GAINS ATTENTION BY BEING CUTE
TRIES TO BE EVERYONE'S FRIEND
OVERPROTECTED BY FAMILY
CHANGES PERSONALITY WITH OTHERS
USUALLY PHYSICALLY SMALLER THAN SIBS
LEARNS TO MANIPULATE FOR WANTS
PROTECTED FROM FAMILY SECRETS

→ ATTEMPT-ACTS AS "CLASS CLOWN"

DEVELOPS ANNOYING COMPULSIONS
PROVIDES COMIC RELIEF IN THE FAMILY

→ GETS AVERAGE GRADES

FEELS INADEQUATE/UNIMPORTANT
MANY ACQUAINTANCES/FEW REAL FRIENDS
PERCEIVED TO TAKE NOTHING SERIOUSLY
FEELS NEVER REALLY LISTENED TO
CAN GET ALONG WITH ALMOST ANYONE
SENSITIVE/TRIES NOT TO SHOW EMOTIONS

→ SMILES WHILE CRYING INSIDE

EXPERIMENTS WITH DRUGS FOR ACCEPTANCE
PROTECTED BY FAMILY FROM PROBLEMS
ACTS YOUNGER THAN HIS AGE/MATURITY
HYPERACTIVE

→ MAY PRESCRIBE
RITALIN

DOESN'T LIKE SILENCE
RUNS FROM ANGER
OTHER ORIENTED
MAY BECOME C.D.
USUALLY MARRIES A HERO
BECOMES DEPENDENT ON SPOUSE
CHILDLIKE "PETER PAN" BEHAVIOR
LACKS SKILLS FOR STRESS
LACKS INTIMACY SKILLS

REALIZATION UNKNOWN TO SELF
MINIMAL ANGER EXPRESSED
PAYOFFS TOO HIGH-FEAR OF LOSS
ROLE IDENTIFIED
GAINS INFO ACoA
MINIMIZES PROBLEMS

→ RELAPSE

FEARS SELF/FEAR OF CRAZINESS

DEALS WITH CONTROL AND PEOPLE-PLEASING
DEALS WITH UNDER-RESPONSIBILITY
TOUCHES ANGER
ADDRESSES CHILD INSIDE
GETS SCARED WITH TRUSTING

DROPS PHONEY FRONT WITH THERAPIST
SOME VALUE CLARIFYING
DEALS WITH DESTRUCTIVE PATTERNS

DEVELOPS FEELING VOCAB

DECEPTION USED
FOR CONTROL

→ RELAPSE

FEELS LOSS
OF CONTROL

RELAPSE

CONDENSED VERSION

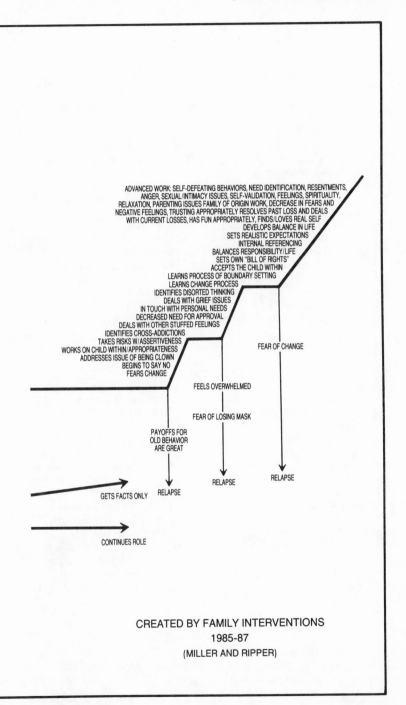

ADVANCED WORK: SELF-DEFEATING BEHAVIORS, NEED IDENTIFICATION, RESENTMENTS, ANGER, SEXUAL/INTIMACY ISSUES, SELF-VALIDATION, FEELINGS, SPIRITUALITY, RELAXATION, PARENTING ISSUES FAMILY OF ORIGIN WORK, DECREASE IN FEARS AND NEGATIVE FEELINGS, TRUSTING APPROPRIATELY RESOLVES PAST LOSS AND DEALS WITH CURRENT LOSSES, HAS FUN APPROPRIATELY, FINDS/LOVES REAL SELF

DEVELOPS BALANCE IN LIFE
SETS REALISTIC EXPECTATIONS
INTERNAL REFERENCING
BALANCES RESPONSIBILITY/LIFE
SETS OWN "BILL OF RIGHTS"
ACCEPTS THE CHILD WITHIN
LEARNS PROCESS OF BOUNDARY SETTING
LEARNS CHANGE PROCESS
IDENTIFIES DISORTED THINKING
DEALS WITH GRIEF ISSUES
IN TOUCH WITH PERSONAL NEEDS
DECREASED NEED FOR APPROVAL
DEALS WITH OTHER STUFFED FEELINGS
IDENTIFIES CROSS-ADDICTIONS
TAKES RISKS W/ASSERTIVENESS
WORKS ON CHILD WITHIN/APPROPRIATENESS
ADDRESSES ISSUE OF BEING CLOWN
BEGINS TO SAY NO
FEARS CHANGE

FEAR OF CHANGE

FEELS OVERWHELMED

FEAR OF LOSING MASK

PAYOFFS FOR
OLD BEHAVIOR
ARE GREAT

GETS FACTS ONLY   RELAPSE   RELAPSE   RELAPSE

CONTINUES ROLE

CREATED BY FAMILY INTERVENTIONS
1985-87
(MILLER AND RIPPER)

N

STEP-BY-STEP PROGRESSION OF THE MASCOT

1. Usually youngest child; baby of the family.
2. Learns to get attention by being cute.
3. Tries to be everyone's friend.
4. Overprotected by family.
5. Changes personality depending on who he/she is with — "chameleon" personality.
6. Usually physically smaller than other siblings.
7. Learns to manipulate passively for what he/she wants.
8. Protected from family secrets.
9. Acts as "Class Clown"/ attempted intervention.
10. Develops annoying mannerisms/ compulsions.
11. Provides comic relief in the family.
12. Gets average grades/attempted intervention.
13. Feels inadequate/unimportant.
14. Has many acquaintances, few real friends.
15. Perceived by others to not take anything seriously.
16. Never really listened to or taken seriously.
17. Has many different types of friends — can get along with most anyone.
18. Afraid of anger/emotions.
19. Is sensitive but never shows emotions.
20. Smiles while crying inside/ attempted intervention.
21. Experiments with alcohol and drugs to be accepted by peers.
22. Protected by family from any problems.
23. Acts younger than his/her age.
24. Always doing something — hyperactive.
25. High incidence of abuse of Ritalin/attempted intervention.
26. Does not like silence.
27. Does not demand anything for self.
28. Has great difficulty in making decisions.
29. Runs from anger.
30. Happiness dependent on others (other-oriented).
31. Uses prescription drugs for nerves.
32. May become dependent on alcohol and/or other drugs.
33. Usually marries a Responsible Child.
34. Becomes very dependent on spouse.
35. Childlike behavior continues — "Peter Pan" person.
36. Lacks communication skills and has trouble understanding.
37. Can't handle daily stress or problems without kidding around or extreme sensitivity.
38. Experiences feelings of going crazy — fears self.

STEP-BY-STEP RECOVERY OF THE MASCOT

1. Seeks help because of feelings of going "crazy".
2. Minimizes problems in therapy — usually does not recognize at this point that he/she is an ACoA.
3. Uses laughter to cover up.
4. In and out of therapy for years.
5. Usually on prescription medications for nerves.
6. Begins to realize that the therapist is taking him/her seriously.
7. Gains education on the family disease concept, ACoA issues.
8. Recognition/identification of family of origin role.
9. Recognition/identification of present day role; minimizes effects of that role.
10. Payoffs too high — fear of loss of defenses, may relapse.
11. Gets scared, fears losing control of the "mask".
12. Identifies ACoA core issues.
13. Expression of minimal anger for not being taken seriously and not being included in family of origin issues.
14. Realization of not knowing who s/he is.
15. Develop a "feeling" vocabulary.
16. Uses vocabulary only on a superficial level but truly believes they are feeling for themselves.
17. Uses deception to continue control.
18. Feels guilty about deception and may drop out of therapy.
19. Backslides, highly other-oriented.
20. Identifies needs met with negative communication skills.
21. Willingness to learn decision-making/handling conflicts.
22. Starts to drop clowning, gets minimal knowledge of self.
23. Learns choicemaking.
24. Values clarification, but with nagging belief that own needs must be sacrificed for others.
25. Starts dropping phoney front (only with therapist).
26. Get's scared with opening up and trusting, feels loss of control.
27. Identifies a war going on between the "child" and the adult inside.
28. Touches on some anger issues.
29. Recognizes under-responsibility.
30. Recognizes control and people-pleasing issues.
31. Recognizes means of escape used in past and present.
32. Fear of change — may relapse.
33. Feelings of hopelessness due to trying new communication and decision-making skills but having no one take him/her seriously.
34. Begins to learn to say "no".
35. Recognizes self-centeredness.
36. Begins working on identifying when the "child" is appropriate and when the "adult" is appropriate.
37. Fear of anger felt towards significant others; fear of insight in self.
38. Takes more risks with assertiveness and being true self/looks at own needs.
39. Realizes what s/he says and does has some value.
40. Identifies cross-addictions.
41. Begins to deal with stuffed feelings.

42. Feels overwhelmed, fears losing control.
43. Possible relapse — fear of losing "mask" and personal control.
44. Decreased need for approval from others.
45. Realizes the price paid for role is not worth the payoff; more in touch with personal needs.
46. Recognizes/identifies personal anger issues and grief issues.
47. Recognizes/identifies old messages.
48. Recognizes/identifies personal loss issues.
49. Identification of distorted thinking and hearing processes.
50. Learns process of change structure.
51. Works through boundaries/ personal conflicts.
52. May relapse, fear of change.
53. Advanced work with self-defeating behaviors.
54. Begins accepting the "child" inside.
55. Identifies and clarifies personal "bill of rights"/advanced needs attainment work.
56. Sets own personal "bill of rights".
57. Begins to identify real self.
58. Takes much more responsibility for own life; sets boundaries.
59. Possible relapse in that they may become over-responsible.
60. Identification of external referencing.
61. Sets unrealistic expectations of self and others.
62. Identifies needs not met in past/ present.
63. Stops taking prescription medications.
64. Deals with anger from past, as well as current anger.
65. Identifies resentments, deals with abandonment issues.
66. Pulls from unhealthy family member(s), shares with other family members.
67. Advanced work on anger issues/ advances grief issues.
68. Works on sexual/incest/abuse issues.
69. Learns relaxation techniques.
70. Develops some balance in daily routine (responsibility, fun, relaxation, human caring).
71. Develops balance in life.
72. Gives self permission to take responsibility.
73. Has fun at appropriate times.
74. Advanced work on self-defeating behaviors.
75. Recognizes real self.
76. Integrates spirituality.
77. Experiences positive "self" feelings.
78. Decides if spouse is wanted in therapy or if spouse wants to be in therapy.
79. Learns appropriate means to gain needs.
80. Has fun appropriately. Works on relationship issues, intimacy issues, parenting issues, self-validation.
81. Becomes able to identify and ask for needs to be met by family and others.
82. Trusts appropriately.
83. Gives self permission to be happy and sets personal future goals.
84. Resolves past and current losses.
85. Finds and loves real self.
86. Breaks cycle.

T

The Wizard (The Enabler)

The foursome continues its journey on the dazzling Yellow Brick Road, singing in unison: "We're off to see the Wizard, the wonderful Wizard of Oz . . ." The Great and Powerful Oz will surely fix things for the "deficient" group. His eminent wisdom and power is reported to be miraculous. In fact, the sentry tells our heroes that the Powerful Oz has things well in control and they need not worry.

As the foursome enters, trembling before him, Oz screams, "Silence! The great and powerful Oz knows why you have come!" The Wizard goes on to verbally abuse each and every member of the group. The Wizard then bellows that he had planned to grant the foursome's requests but that they must first perform a very small errand. To gain their requests, they are commanded to bring back to Oz the broomstick of the Wicked Witch of the West.

Just as the Wizard created a "crisis" for the foursome to master, so, too, does the family Enabler. Enablers create crises so they can rescue victims and gain praise and respect. Children in the crisis also attempt to master the crisis to gain praise and increase their self-worth within the family. The lure of carrying out the Enabler's commands is the hope of being truly "worthy" and obtaining their "requests" (needs).

Ironically, as Enablers, we truly believe we can provide solutions by means of control. This distorted thinking process enables us to continue in the belief that we have the power to change the sickness that entraps the family. Despite the belief that we have all the answers, we feel as helpless and hopeless as the Wizard felt without his frightening mask and protective curtain. The Wizard's costume kept him protected from facing reality. Similarly, we wear masks of denial, control and martyrdom so we will not have to face our own vulnerability and reality. Most of us believe that if we become vulnerable, we will lose all control and be destroyed.

The focus of the Enabler is constantly on others — spouse, children, sisters, etc. Once again, focusing on others keeps the pressure off. This hinders any *personal* recovery process. As long as the focus is placed on another person, the Enabler can continue dysfunctional behavior.

Common Characteristics of the Enabler

- We act out of loyalty to the family.
- We don't see any choices for different behaviors.
- We can usually deal with any crisis.
- We feel tired physically and emotionally.
- We smooth over embarrassment.
- We take over the alcoholic's responsibilities, jobs, etc.
- We play saver and caretaker.

- We skimp on budgets, do without, save burdens and guilt from dependent.
- We appear to be discouraging the drinking.
- We prevent crises by not allowing the dependent to "hit bottom".
- We get payoffs through forms of admiration with comments such as, "How *do* you do it?"
- We are often resentful, angry, guilty, self-hating.
- We feel isolated.
- We turn off our feelings.
- High rate of stress-related illnesses (ulcers, headaches, colitis, depression, etc.).
- High incidence of poor nutrition, too much smoking, overweight.
- High incidence of tranquilizer abuse.
- We need to deal with sexual issues (frigidity, lack of sexual fulfillment, etc.).
- We feel powerless.
- We seek help, mostly though medical doctors, for physical ailments.

The Enabler has been given (and takes) most responsibility for the family. Our misplaced emphasis is on taking control of the alcoholic or the dysfunctional person. It is a constant struggle, not only to keep the family together, but to create family harmony. In this attempt, we disassociate with any positives we once saw within ourselves and in the family. This disassociation happens as a result of the following:

1. Focus is put on the alcoholic and/or dysfunctional person.
2. There is a constant struggle for perfection.
3. Peace must be maintained at all costs.
4. A protection device is commonly used.

1. Focusing on the Alcoholic and/or Dysfunctional Person

Because we came from a home that was dysfunctional, long ago we made a vow to ourselves that *OUR* family

H

would be different. Our family would be a family without problems. If a problem did arise, we would work together as a team toward a resolution. This ideal was probably ingrained by the different media forms. Television brought us *Father Knows Best, The Donna Reed Show, The Brady Bunch, Leave it to Beaver,* etc. Fairy tales and movies brought us *Cinderella, Snow White, Lady and the Tramp, Gone With the Wind,* etc. Then of course there are the romance novels we read as teenagers and some of us continue to read as adults. For some of us, watching and listening to these media forms was the only way we had of comparing what we were experiencing to what we wanted as adults.

Another media form that has affected us all is music. We probably reminisce about who we were dating or what was happening in our lives when a particular old song is played. We compulsively would buy that record and play it over and over again. Fantasizing is an important element in our lives, but we didn't know how to put it into perspective. Unfortunately, we also may not have known how to choose the right people to help make our dreams come true.

When we realize that our fantasies are not becoming realities, we look for the reasons why. The "Why?" is answered by our alcoholic. "If it wasn't for _____, everything would be great around here." We set out to make everything wonderful by fixing what we see as the problem: namely, our alcoholic or dysfunctional person. Unfortunately, when a problem occurs, we have been taught to fix it by becoming responsible. The way we become responsible is to focus on the problem, take charge of the problem (control it), and fix it. It doesn't matter whether or not it's ours to fix.

We find ourselves obsessed with our alcoholic, trying everything we know to alter his/her drinking or behaviors. We accuse, blame, shame and even at times take on the philosophy, "If you can't beat 'em, join 'em." We then see ourselves as failures because we can't change the other person. We learned these fixing methods as children, watching our parents. Other fixing methods were internalized by watching methods that were used on us. These methods probably worked in altering our behavior as children. Our parents' methods worked, so we assume that they should work for everyone else. It's very puzzling for us when our methods don't work and we, therefore, assume that we must be doing something wrong . . . again.

2. The Constant Struggle for Perfection

The majority of Enablers grew up in dysfunctional families as the Responsible Child. Our desire for perfection began in our role as the Responsible Child and now, as adults, we attempt to perfect our perfectionism. Our need for perfectionism began long before we got married and it is one of the reasons we chose the dysfunctional mate we did.

Even our fantasies are based on the "perfect" family. We look for the "perfect" solution and spend hours planning the "perfect" method of resolution. Unfortunately, for a number of reasons, we don't get the results we desire.

1. There *is* no perfect solution, so we spend all of our time looking for something that is not available.
2. By the time we find the perfect solution the problem has either been resolved or we have spent so much time perfecting our method we have lost our energy to follow through.
3. The perfect solution is never set into motion because we think there is an even better method of handling the situation.
4. We attempt the resolution and don't get the results we are seeking so we blame ourselves (shame) for not having the perfect answer. The

end result is usually that the problem does not get resolved, unless it resolves itself.

In a dysfunctional family, perfectionism is increased by overcompensating for the alcoholic. If the spouse is seen as becoming more irresponsible, we become more responsible. If we see him/her as less communicative, we become more communicative. This happens in all areas of our lives. Basically, we tend to overcompensate by doing the extreme opposite of any action taken by the alcoholic.

Figure 3.5. Couple's Balancing Chart.

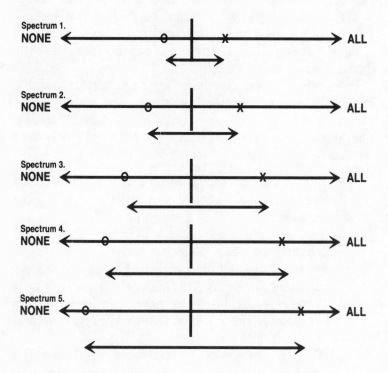

Spectrum 1: This shows how a couple will interact prior to marriage. Responsibility, communication and feelings toward one another are usually shared equally.

Spectrum 2: Distancing begins. One person in the relationship begins to withdraw slightly from participation within the relationship. The other person attempts to compensate by slightly increasing his/her responsibilities.

Spectrum 3: Distancing gradually and constantly increases with "O" giving up more and more responsibility and communicating less and less. The compensation continues by "X" gradually and constantly taking what "O" has given up. "X" assumes the responsibilities with little questioning due to three factors: (1) the process is gradually enabling "X" to make only minor changes regularly, (2) "X" is the Enabler, and compensating is seen as part of what is expected, and (3) the number of crises is increasing, giving "X" self-rationalizations to assume more and more responsibility.

Spectrum 4: "X" now begins feeling and recognizing all the extra responsibility. With the recognition comes feelings of anger and resentment, which are passively expressed to "O". Or "X" will express feelings aggressively without giving any consequences or by using idle threats. "O" will not only continue the non-participation, it will increase due to having no reason (no real consequences) to change. "O" will have inward feelings of being controlled, not being allowed to participate, being the "bad guy" and resentment.

Spectrum 5: "X" feels overwhelmed, in a constant crisis and usually decides that something needs to be done. "O" feels totally dominated, hopeless and helpless.

3. Peace At All Costs

One major problem that the Enabler faces in dealing with situations is that of trying not to rock the boat. We look for solutions to problems to avoid someone getting upset or angry with us. Because of this fear of anger, we do not approach situations head on. Instead, we always attempt to resolve them by "coming in through the back door" (using a passive style).

We have learned that if we use the indirect approach, it severely limits our alternatives and usually places all the responsibility on us. In doing so, not only do we fail to obtain the desired results, but we also feel abandoned by significant others who do not give us the support we are seeking. Another problem that results in using a passive style is that we feel our family does not listen to us, understand us or understand the situation. This leads to resentment, anger and feelings of abandonment.

4. Protection Device

Our role as an Enabler is a very visible role. It leaves us open to being hurt, so we need many layers of armor to protect ourselves. This armor shields us from the hurt and does not let the outside world in. Likewise this shield does not let us come out into the world of reality. It stops us from seeing the world and ourselves as they really exist. This shield not only stops the negative feelings from penetrating, but it unfortunately blocks the positive feelings which we so desperately need.

The armor for the shield consists of over-responsibility, intellectualizing, denying and passivity. This is the only way we have learned to handle the situations and to avoid pain. The irony is that using this shield causes us more pain.

The Positive Side of The Enabler

The Wizard stands, humbled, before the foursome. He has decided that HE must take the situation in hand and personally take Dorothy to Kansas. Feeling quite proud and dignified, the Wizard states that he will face any catastrophic event to return poor Dorothy to her farmhouse in Kansas. The Wizard denies his existence as the Great and Powerful Oz and drops his phoney facade to show his vulnerabilities and love to the group.

When we drop the phoney mask of caretaker, we allow our vulnerability and love to emerge, just as the Wizard did. With that change, Enablers can see the positive characteristics that we hold within. All that was needed was to focus within, instead of looking beyond our own backyards.

Before you read on, write down the positives that have been developed and learned as a result of this role. It doesn't matter if this is your role or not. Look at the strengths of the role. (Please do not feel limited by the numbering.)

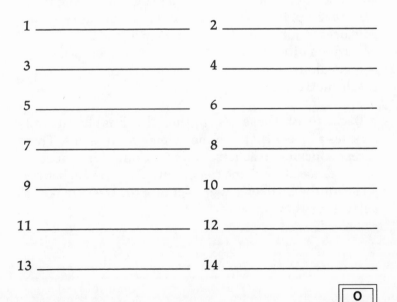

1 _____   2 _____

3 _____   4 _____

5 _____   6 _____

7 _____   8 _____

9 _____   10 _____

11 _____   12 _____

13 _____   14 _____

O

Here are Some of Your Positives

THE ENABLER . . .

is organized
is self-reliant
is punctual
is a good worker
is loyal
is compassionate
is a good listener
trusts self with tasks
pays attention to details
is excellent in a crisis
is a high achiever
is mature
is logical/reasonable
wants to do the best job
has stamina
has self-control
honors commitments
has high morals/values
is a good supervisor
has longevity in a job
advances in jobs quickly
gives good directions
is meticulous
is self-motivating

is reliable
is dependable
finishes tasks
has leadership qualities
makes decisions
is tenacious
is sensitive to others
is introspective
is responsible
is civic-minded
is strong willed
follows orders
gets results on projects
is thrifty
is a hard worker
is honest
is competitive
is very spiritual
is a good housekeeper
has a good memory
implements ideas
has a high tolerance
follows rules

Because of these strengths, the Enabler usually chooses a career that is in the helping professions. These careers include teachers, nurses, counselors, doctors, lawyers, social workers, clergy, etc. They are high stress jobs, but the Enabler's high tolerance for stress makes us perfect for these careers.

Place within this mask of the Wizard the positives that you possess from this role. Include with an asterisk (*) the characteristics you desire to integrate into your journey.

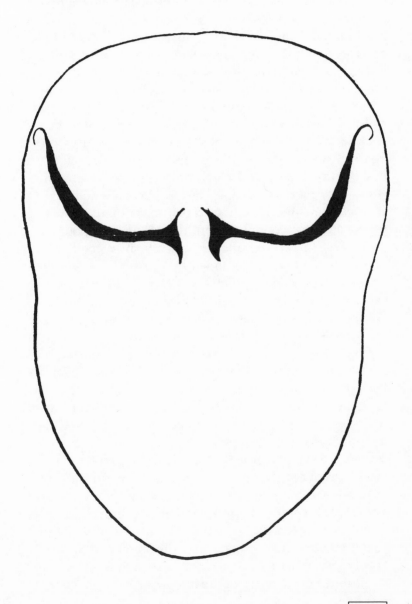

The Progression and Recovery of The Enabler

As Enablers, we gained our training as children in our families of origin. We then continue our enabling role in our own adult lives. We have successfully learned to be comfortable with the inappropriate behavior of others, as well as maintain our shame in thinking that the inappropriate behavior is *our* fault. Our shame maintenance keeps us locked into low self-esteem, doubt in our abilities, "black and white" decisions and self-abuse.

Despite our repeated vows to never be "in this mess again", we find ourselves once again drawn to a dysfunctional person. In fact, not only are we drawn to these dysfunctional people, but we become addicted to the relationship. To our distress, most of us decide to marry a dysfunctional person, thus continuing our self-destructive pain and shame. Despite our good intentions, we find we are trapped by our own destruction. Our pain and broken promises of change allow others to create our destinies. We become helpless and hopeless (as we were as children), falling deeper and deeper into our bottomless pit of despair.

When we can no longer accept the pain, we begin to address our anger and begin a struggle for survival. As we struggle, we realize that our "bottoming out" has forced us to address our OWN behaviors. We are forced to look at ourselves, despite our desire to "fix" our dysfunctional family member.

Denial is a key factor that needs to be addressed early in our recovery. Many of us get detoured in our early journey because we take the focus off ourselves and once again center it on someone or something else. Some of us get caught in the trap of denial and think that we may have exaggerated the dysfunction in our family. Some of us learn about our enabling role, but continue old patterns because of our fear of change.

U

This is indicated in the Progression and Recovery Chart (Figure 3.6) by the circling of our progress along our first major advancement. Many of us stay in that circling pattern for weeks, months or years because of our inability to face reality. Anger, despair, hopelessness and helplessness return if we don't address our issues of control, martyrism and over-responsibility.

We need to look at the payoffs for our enabling before we can continue on our journey. After we address the payoffs and realize our inability to change others, we continue onward along our path. There is dramatic progress when we discover that the journey is truly for ourselves. Once we come to that realization, we begin to believe in our abilities and feel confident that we can deal with the anger, grief and loss. Our lives become our own for the first time and we start to find out that we have things called *needs*.

With this revelation, we start to learn that we can meet our own needs without giving up ourselves. We discover that we do not need to control everything and everyone around us for approval. As we set boundaries for ourselves, we begin to find the true person who has been hiding deep within.

Figure 3.6.

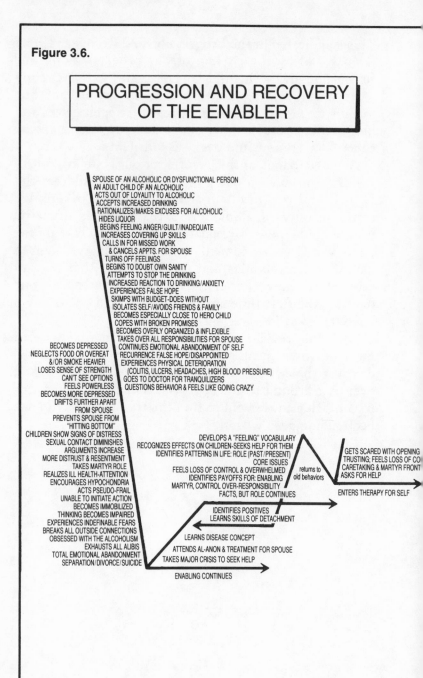

PROGRESSION AND RECOVERY OF THE ENABLER

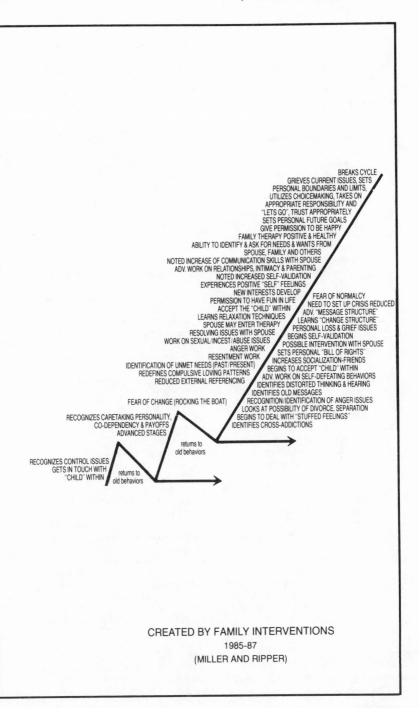

BREAKS CYCLE
GRIEVES CURRENT ISSUES, SETS
PERSONAL BOUNDARIES AND LIMITS,
UTILIZES CHOICEMAKING, TAKES ON
APPROPRIATE RESPONSIBILITY AND
"LETS GO", TRUST APPROPRIATELY
SETS PERSONAL FUTURE GOALS
GIVE PERMISSION TO BE HAPPY
FAMILY THERAPY POSITIVE & HEALTHY
ABILITY TO IDENTIFY & ASK FOR NEEDS & WANTS FROM
SPOUSE, FAMILY AND OTHERS
NOTED INCREASE OF COMMUNICATION SKILLS WITH SPOUSE
ADV. WORK ON RELATIONSHIPS, INTIMACY & PARENTING
NOTED INCREASED SELF-VALIDATION
EXPERIENCES POSITIVE "SELF" FEELINGS
NEW INTERESTS DEVELOP
PERMISSION TO HAVE FUN IN LIFE
ACCEPT THE "CHILD" WITHIN
LEARNS RELAXATION TECHNIQUES
SPOUSE MAY ENTER THERAPY
RESOLVING ISSUES WITH SPOUSE
WORK ON SEXUAL/INCEST/ABUSE ISSUES
ANGER WORK
RESENTMENT WORK
IDENTIFICATION OF UNMET NEEDS (PAST/PRESENT)
REDEFINES COMPULSIVE LOVING PATTERNS
REDUCED EXTERNAL REFERENCING

FEAR OF NORMALCY
NEED TO SET UP CRISIS REDUCED
ADV. "MESSAGE STRUCTURE"
LEARNS "CHANGE STRUCTURE"
PERSONAL LOSS & GRIEF ISSUES
BEGINS SELF-VALIDATION
POSSIBLE INTERVENTION WITH SPOUSE
SETS PERSONAL "BILL OF RIGHTS"
INCREASES SOCIALIZATION-FRIENDS
BEGINS TO ACCEPT "CHILD" WITHIN
ADV. WORK ON SELF-DEFEATING BEHAVIORS
IDENTIFIES DISTORTED THINKING & HEARING
IDENTIFIES OLD MESSAGES
RECOGNITION/IDENTIFICATION OF ANGER ISSUES
LOOKS AT POSSIBILITY OF DIVORCE, SEPARATION
BEGINS TO DEAL WITH "STUFFED FEELINGS"
IDENTIFIES CROSS-ADDICTIONS

FEAR OF CHANGE (ROCKING THE BOAT)

RECOGNIZES CARETAKING PERSONALITY,
CO-DEPENDENCY & PAYOFFS
ADVANCED STAGES

returns to
old behaviors

RECOGNIZES CONTROL ISSUES
GETS IN TOUCH WITH
"CHILD" WITHIN

returns to
old behaviors

CREATED BY FAMILY INTERVENTIONS
1985-87
(MILLER AND RIPPER)

STEP-BY-STEP PROGRESSION OF THE ENABLER

1. Usually the spouse of an alcoholic.
2. Usually an Adult Child of an Alcoholic.
3. Acts out of loyalty to the alcoholic.
4. Accepts increased drinking quietly.
5. Rationalizes spouse's increase in drinking.
6. Makes excuses for the alcoholic.
7. Starts to hide the liquor.
8. Begins to feel angry and guilty about not being a good enough wife/husband.
9. Becomes more and more competent at covering up embarrassments.
10. Calls in for missed work and cancels appointments for spouse.
11. Turns off feelings.
12. Begins to doubt own sanity.
13. Appears to be trying to stop the drinking.
14. Continuously reacts to drinking and feelings of anxiety.
15. Experiences false hope.
16. Skimps on budget, does without.
17. Isolates self from and avoids friends and family.
18. Becomes especially close to Responsible Child.
19. Copes with broken promises, becomes overly organized and inflexible.
20. Takes over all responsibilities for spouse.
21. Experiences physical deterioration: colitis, ulcers, headaches, high blood pressure.
22. Goes to a doctor for stress-related illness, usually given tranquilizers.
23. Begins to question behavior and feels like he/she is going crazy.
24. Neglects food or becomes overweight, may smoke heavily.
25. Loses willpower.
26. Can't see options/black and white thinking.
27. Feels powerless.
28. Drifts further away from spouse.
29. Trust declines.
30. Prevents spouse's crisis of "hitting bottom".
31. Children begin to show definite signs of emotional distress.
32. Sexual contact with spouse diminishes.
33. Arguments increase in the home.
34. Becomes more distrustful and resentful.
35. Neglects own needs.
36. Gets payoffs by playing the martyr.
37. Ill health gets attention; encourages hypochondria.
38. Controls more; takes on more responsibility.
39. Acts pseudo-frail.
40. Higher tolerance for inappropriate actions of others.
41. Unable to initiate action.
42. Becomes immobilized.
43. Thinking becomes impaired.
44. Experiences indefinable fears.
45. Pulls away from final connection to the outside — the church.
46. If wife is Enabler, will stay with alcoholic 9 out of 10 times if there are children under 10.
47. If husband is the Enabler, will stay with alcoholic wife 1 out of 10 times.
48. Threatens to get outside help.
49. Becomes obsessed with spouse's alcoholism.
50. Exhausts all alibis.
51. Assumes total responsibility for family.
52. Avoids all sexual contact.
53. Low self-esteem.
54. Admits defeat/feels outside self.
55. Separation or divorce.

STEP-BY-STEP RECOVERY OF THE ENABLER

1. Generally, around seven-year mark seeks outside help at crisis.
2. Attends Al-Anon or treatment.
3. Joins Al-Anon and treatment for others only (spouse).
4. Learns disease concept.
5. Learns skills of detachment.
6. Breaks some denial or relapses.
7. Looks at payoffs of enabling: martyr, control, over-responsibility.
8. Feels the loss of control.
9. Feels overwhelmed with issues.
10. Awareness of being an ACoA, dysfunctional issues.
11. Looks at problems of attraction to spouse.
12. Recognizes needs of children.
13. Seeks treatment for children (could be decoy to drop therapy or to get external referencing).
14. Gains education on the concept of Adult Child issues.
15. Recognition of role played in family of origin.
16. Recognition/identification of present day role and another look at payoffs.
17. Quick, superficial therapeutic gains; motivation for recovery high.
18. Establishes a beginning support structure through Al-Anon or an ACoA group.
19. Identifies ACoA core issues.
20. Develops a "feeling" vocabulary.
21. Learns communication skills, decision-making and values clarification.
22. Overwhelmed with issues, feels loss of control.
23. Black/white extremes dealing with core issues.
24. Begins to identify parenting issues.
25. Identification of rigid structure of parenting.
26. Backslide, other-oriented.
27. Enters therapy for self.
28. Asks for help.
29. Starts to look at caretaking, martyr front.
30. Gets scared with opening up, trusting; feels loss of control.
31. Gets in touch with the "child" inside.
32. Recognizes over-responsible role.
33. Fear of change, fear of abandonment; may relapse.
34. Recognizes control issues.
35. Fear of change, may relapse.
36. Recognizes caretaking personality, co-dependency and payoffs — advanced stage.
37. Fear of change (rocking the boat); may relapse.
38. Identifies cross-addictions (compulsive loving, over-spending, eating disorders, etc.).
39. Identifies losses of past.
40. Begins to deal with stuffed feelings.
41. Looks at possibility of divorce, separation.
42. Identifies boundaries — risks letting go of some responsibility.
43. Feelings of being overwhelmed, fear of loss of control.
44. Recognition/identification of personal anger issues.
45. Identification of old messages.
46. Identification of distorted thinking and hearing processes.
47. Learns to trust others and ask for help selectively.
48. Advanced work on self-defeating behaviors.
49. Learns choicemaking.

50. Begins to accept the "child" inside.
51. Deals with fear of abandonment, hurt, anger.
52. Increases socialization, friends.
53. Own needs identified.
54. Learns to say "No".
55. Sets personal "bill of rights".
56. Possible intervening techniques with spouse.
57. Regains emotional stability, self-esteem.
58. Recognition/identification of personal loss and grief issues.
59. Sets boundaries for responsibility.
60. Learns process of "change structure".
61. Redefinition of "message structure".
62. Identifies need not to set up a crisis/advanced work on abandonment issues.
63. Fear of normalcy and calmness.
64. Identification of external referencing.
65. Redefines compulsive loving pattern.
66. Identification of unmet needs, past and present.
67. Addresses spirituality.
68. Increased accuracy in identifying feelings.
69. Identifies resentments.
70. Identifies anger.
71. Identifies and addresses sexual or incest/abuse issues.
72. Works through some issues with spouse, forgiving, or spouse may join therapy.
73. Learns relaxation techniques/allows self to have fun.
74. Accepts the "child" within.
75. Starts to know real self.
76. Self-validation, self-affirmation.
77. Grieves past losses and addresses current losses.
78. Gives self permission to have fun.
79. New interests develop, perhaps job or schooling.
80. Experiences positive "self" feelings.
81. Noted increased self-worth, self-esteem.
82. Integrates spirituality.
83. Mourns past losses (grief work).
84. Work on relationship issues, intimacy issues, parenting issues.
85. Communication skills with spouse better.
86. Able to identify _and_ ask for needs and wants from spouse and others.
87. Family therapy more positive/healthy.
88. Gives self permission to be happy and set personal future goals.
89. Breaks cycle.

H

THERAPEUTIC ISSUES

Many Enablers are disliked by therapists who do not have the patience needed to help us through our journey. Many therapists do not understand the reasons for our resistance to change and our fear of the unknown. Therapists do not know the anger and resentments that we hold inside. Unfortunately, many unknowing professionals deal with our issues of enabling without addressing our home-of-origin issues. This is because many therapists see only our symptoms, and not the causes of our dysfunction. Because of that error, many of us deal with the immediate crisis and break from our current dysfunctional person, but continue the self-destruction within our next relationship. This in turn causes us to unknowingly question our sanity and our abilities of self-direction.

Recovery is static for us. We go up and down in our early-to-middle recovery program like a yo-yo. Each up-and-down movement, however, makes us stronger and more capable of facing the next issue and the next risk.

As we move along our recovery path, the therapist must be able to deal with our stuffed anger and resentments which we have held inside for so long. Our anger and resentment has taught us that we are not capable of relationships or love. We feel numb and incapable of joy. We have isolated ourselves from others and do not know how to reach out and ask for help. We have no concept of what our needs are or how to get them met in a healthy manner. Fun is an unknown commodity to us. We must also learn how to parent our children in a healthy way, as we start to "parent" ourselves. For most of us, we need to take away the critical parent that lives within us and constantly demands our perfection.

As we journey down the path we need many skills, but we are quick learners because we truly desire a change that makes a lifetime difference!

4

The Balloon Leaves For Kansas

(Treatment Issues)

The Residents of the Emerald City watch in amazement as the balloon that was supposed to carry Dorothy to her destination carried the dismayed Wizard upward alone. The Scarecrow, Tin Man and Cowardly Lion tell Dorothy that she should stay with them because they love her! She feels desperately caught between her need to go back and the temptation to stay with her loving friends. Despite this pull, she knows that Kansas would never be the same, even if she could return.

Dorothy knew that she would never be able to be the same person after her experiences in Oz. You, too, know that you are not the same person you were at the beginning of your recovery. As we know, going back means our own self-destruction.

Glenda gave Dorothy the gift of believing in her self — we are giving you the means of finding your own path home! Provided below are treatment plans for the continuation of your journey to integration:

1

FEELINGS

Feelings are the means of developing intimacy with people; for, without feelings we remain isolated. Because we have numbed ourselves, we first need to learn how to identify what we are feeling and put it into words by having a "feeling vocabulary". Feelings are like alcoholism. When an alcoholic returns to drinking, the drinking begins at the point that it stopped. This is also true for feelings, but don't let this scare you. Unlike alcoholism, you can work through these uncomfortable feelings to find the feelings that you have been looking to experience.

Enabler:
1) Develop a Feelings Vocabulary
2) Identify Feelings
3) Express Feelings

Responsible Child:
1) Develop a Feelings Vocabulary
2) Identify Feelings
3) Express Feelings

Lost Child:
1) Develop a Feelings Vocabulary
2) Identify Feelings
3) Express Feelings

Scapegoat:
1) Develop a Feelings Vocabulary
2) Identify Feelings
3) Express Feelings

Mascot:
1) Develop a Feelings Vocabulary
2) Identify Feelings
3) Express Feelings

TRUST

We have difficulty trusting because we were taught not to trust when we were little. This can be scary, but remember you DON'T have to trust EVERYONE.

Enabler:
1) How To Trust
2) Who To Trust
3) Who Not To Trust
4) Develop Trusting Relationships

Responsible
Child:
1) How To Trust
2) Who To Trust
3) Who Not To Trust
4) Develop Trusting Relationships

Lost Child:
1) How To Trust
2) Who To Trust
3) Who Not To Trust
4) Develop Trusting Relationships

Scapegoat:
1) How To Trust
2) Who To Trust
3) Develop Trusting Relationships

(The Scapegoat knows who not to trust)

Mascot:
1) How To Trust
2) Who To Trust
3) Who Not To Trust
4) Develop Trusting Relationships

SELF-CARE

We have been taught to take care of ourselves by protecting with a suit of armor. Unfortunately, this did not allow us to get to know ourselves and what we want. Now it is time for us to learn what we want and how to take care of our needs, while obtaining them in a fulfilling manner.

Enabler: 1) Identify Values
Responsible   2) Learn How to Maintain Values
Child: 3) Identifying Needs
Lost Child: 4) Learn How to Obtain Needs
                5) Learn Responsibility for Self

6) Learn "Bill of Rights"
7) Learn How to Obtain Rights
8) Learn Internal Orientation versus External
9) Learn Self-validation
10) Learn to Identification of Positives

Scapegoat:
1) Identify Values
2) Learn How to Maintain Values
3) Identify Needs
4) Learn How to Maintain Needs
5) Learn How to Take Responsibility
6) Learn Responsibility for Self
7) Learn "Bill of Rights"
8) Learn How to Obtain Rights
9) Learn Internal Orientation versus External
10) Learn Self-validation
11) Learn to Identify Positives
12) Learn Self-management Skills

Mascot:
1) Identify Values
2) Learn How to Maintain Values
3) Identify Needs
4) Learn How to Obtain Needs
5) Learn How to Take Responsibility
6) Learn How to Take Responsibility for Self
7) Learn "Bill of Rights"
8) Learn How to Obtain Rights
9) Learn Internal Orientation
10) Learn Self-validation
11) Learn Identification of Positives
12) Learn Self-management Skills

RELATIONSHIPS

The thing that we are always crying out for is a relationship, but we never seem to obtain the relation-

N

ships we desire. Relationships can be rewarding and meet our needs, but we need to LEARN how to develop a healthy relationship with healthy people.

Responsible Child:
1) Identify Different Types of Relationships
2) Identify Realistic Expectations

Enabler:
3) Identify Needs
4) Learn How to Ask for Needs
5) Learn Intimacy
6) Identify Boundaries
7) Identify Loving Patterns
8) Learn Communication Skills
9) Learn How to Identify Healthy People
10) Learn How to Interact with Healthy People
11) Learn Fair Fighting Rules
12) Learn How to Compromise
13) Learn to Accept Compliments
14) Learn to Say "No"
15) Learn to Identify Anger Issues
16) Learn to Express Anger Appropriately
17) Learn to Identify Issues
18) Learn to Confront Issues
19) Learn to Hear Feedback from Others
20) Learn to Critique Feedback from Others
21) Learn Not to Take Responsibility for Others
22) Identify Rights
23) Learn How to Acquire Rights within a Relationship

Lost Child:
1) Identify Different Types of Relationships
2) Learn How to Approach People
3) Learn How to Converse Within a Group

4) Learn to Feel Comfortable Within a Group
5) Identify Realistic Expectations
6) Identify Needs
7) Learn How to Obtain Needs
8) Learn Intimacy
9) Identify Loving Patterns
10) Learn Boundaries
11) Learn Communication Skills
12) Learn to Identify Healthy People
13) Learn to Interact with Healthy People
14) Identify Rights Within a Relationship
15) Learn How to Obtain and Maintain Rights
16) Learn to Compromise Without Giving Up Rights
17) Learn to Hear Compliments
18) Learn to Accept Compliments
19) Learn to Say "No"
20) Identify Anger Issues
21) Learn to Express Anger
22) Learn Fair Fighting Rules
23) Learn to Identify Issues
24) Learn to Confront Issues
25) Learn to Hear Feedback from Others
26) Learn to Critique Feedback from Others
27) Learn Not to Take Responsibility for Others

Scapegoat: 1) Identify Different Types of Relationships
2) Identify Realistic Expectations
3) Identify Needs
4) Learn How to Obtain Needs in a Healthy Style
5) Learn Intimacy
6) Identify Loving Patterns

7) Learn Boundaries
8) Learn Communication Skills
9) Learn to Identify Healthy People
10) Learn to Interact with Healthy People
11) Identify Rights Within a Relationship
12) Learn to Maintain Rights in a Healthy Style
13) Learn Compromising Skills
14) Learn to Accept Compliments
15) Learn to Say "Yes"
16) Identify Anger Issues
17) Learn Positive Styles of Expressing Anger
18) Learn Fair Fighting Rules
19) Learn to Identify Issues
20) Learn to Express Issues in a Healthy Style
21) Learn to Hear Feedback from Others
22) Learn to Critique Feedback from Others

Mascot: Same as Enabler and Responsible Child plus:
23) Learn How to be Serious in a Relationship

OLD MESSAGES

We are filled with old messages that were given to us either by significant others or ourselves. These old messages can be very self-destructive in many ways. We need to identify these messages and alter them to work for us instead of against us. Note that the word *alter* was used and not *discard*. There may be some messages that you will want to totally discard, but many more may just need to be altered.

T

Enabler, Lost Child, Scapegoat, Mascot and Responsible Child:	1) Identify Old Messages 2) Identify Behaviors Required to Maintain Old Messages 3) Identify Behaviors Not Allowed 4) Identify Consequences of Behaviors 5) Identify Payoffs of Behaviors 6) Identify Desired Messages 7) Identify Behaviors to Achieve Messages 8) Identify Payoffs 9) Identify Consequences 10) Learn to Integrate Desired Behaviors and Messages

DECISION-MAKING

So you wonder what stops us from getting problems solved or what almost immobilizes us when we are faced with choices and decisions? Most of the time, we can handle a crisis without thinking twice. However, we never learned the decision-making process. We need to learn this process in order to make sound rational decisions that are in our best interests.

Decision-making is an important part of everyday life. Most decisions are made without thinking. Others are avoided. Life can become much easier when we learn how to make good decisions.

Enabler, Responsible Child, Lost Child:	1) Identify Old Messages about Decision-Making 2) Use New Message Process with Destructive Messages 3) Learn Decision-Making Process 4) Identify Where Process is Breaking Down 5) Identify Short-Term Goals 6) Identify Long-Term Goals 7) Learn How to Implement Goals

8) Learn to Take Risks
9) Learn to Broaden Base of Options
10) Learn to Recognize Consequences
11) Learn Undistorted Reality
12) Learn It's Okay to Make a Mistake
13) Learn to Value Instincts
14) Learn How to Prioritize

Scapegoat and Mascot:

1) Identify Old Messages about Decision-Making
2) Use New Message Process with Destructive Messages
3) Learn Decision-Making Process
4) Identify Where Process is Breaking Down
5) Identify Short-Term Goals
6) Identify Long-Term Goals
7) Learn How to Implement Goals
8) Learn to Recognize Consequences of Risks
9) Learn to Broaden Base of Options
10) Learn to Recognize Consequences
11) Learn Undistorted Reality
12) Learn It's Okay to Make a Mistake
13) Learn to Value Own Instincts
14) Learn How to Prioritize

PLAY

Play is an essential part of life. Play give us the mental rest we need to be productive with the rest of our waking hours. Most of us were given the message when we were children that we were irresponsible when we played. Now, when we take time out to play, we can almost feel Mom or Dad sitting on our shoulder telling us that we should be using our time doing something productive. As a result, we may not allow ourselves to play. When we do, we are busy feeling guilty about what we should be doing; thus, we do not enjoy our play time.

Play comes in many forms; from long vacations, to weekends away, to the five-minute break at work. How many of us return home from a vacation and feel like we never left? We often go into work on Monday morning and can't believe we just had two days off. For some of us, the only way we feel that we can take time off is when we are sick. Of course, we have to be *very* sick to take a day off of work! Stress, or the lack of it, plays a very important part in our health. If we don't play occasionally, we will get sick. We *need* a mental rest during the day and a week or two of vacation during the year.

For those of us who have difficulty playing, the first step is to tell ourselves that this time *is productive*. It allows us to use the rest of the day in a productive manner. Then we need to look at the messages that we were given as children about play, redefine those messages and develop methods to enact new messages. In this way, we can learn how to play and use play to help us throughout the year.

Responsible Enabler:
1) Learn How to Play
2) Learn What I Enjoy For Fun
3) Learn to Develop Fun Relationships and Have Fun within Current Relationships
4) Give Self Permission to Have Fun
5) Learn Relaxation Skills
6) Learn to Enjoy Time Alone
7) Learn to Take Vacations without Taking Reality Along
8) Learn How to Take Mini-Vacations
9) Develop a Sense of Humor
10) Develop Flexibility
11) Develop Spontaneity

Lost Child:
1) Learn How to Play with Others
2) Learn What I Enjoy for Fun

E

    3) Learn to Develop Fun Relationships and Have Fun in Current Relationships

    4) Learn to Give Self Permission to Have Fun with Others

    5) Learn Relaxation Skills

    6) Develop a Sense of Humor

    7) Develop Spontaneity

Scapegoat and Mascot:

    1) Learn to Play in a Self-enhancing Style

    2) Learn What I Enjoy for Fun

    3) Learn to Develop Fun Relationships and Having Fun within Current Relationships

    4) Learn Moderation in Having Fun

    5) Learn Relaxation Skills

    6) Learn to Enjoy Time Alone

    7) Learn How to Make Transition from Fun to Responsibility

FAMILY SKILLS

When we think of being a part of a family, we usually don't think in terms of needing skills. Society has taught us that a male should know how to be a husband and father because he is male, and a female should know how to be a wife and mother because she is female. If we have problems within our family, we look at it as our fault — we are not doing our job as a male or female.

Thirty to forty years ago the male and female roles were clearly defined. We knew what to expect and what was expected of us as wives and mothers or as husbands and fathers. These roles have changed as our society has changed. Also a couple did not raise children by themselves. They had the help of grandparents, neighbors, the community church and the schools. Today a family is virtually left on its own. The high number of "broken" homes with only one parent and the involvement of many "steps" (step-parents) only complicates matters further. We are confused as to what our rights are as parents, step-parents, grandparents, teachers and neighbors. Add to this our confusion as to what is expected of us as wives or husbands and we can see why the family is in danger these days. Usually there is nobody around to help us gain needed skills.

A number of us told ourselves that our families would be different than the ones we grew up in. Did we accomplish this or are we just repeating the past (or the exact opposite, which can be just as destructive)?

Enabler,	1) Learn Parenting Skills
Responsible	2) Learn to Set Limits for Children
Child	3) Learn to Be Consistent
Scapegoat,	4) Learn the Elements and Behaviors of
Mascot	Healthy Families
and	5) Learn to Play as a Family
Lost Child:	6) Identify Family Goals
	7) Learn Intimacy within the Family
	8) Identify Boundaries within a Family
	9) Learn How to Be Supportive
	10) Learn How to Have Individual Relationships within the Family

THE CHILD INSIDE

The child inside is very important to us as adults. It hold the playful side of us, the side that allows spontaneity, the non-serious side, the loving side, the light humorous side of us, the side that allows us to play with our children in a healthy, playful manner. This child has usually been ignored and at times feared.

Enabler,	1) Learn to Get in Touch with the Child
Responsible	Inside
Child,	2) Identify Losses of the Child
Scapegoat,	3) Learn to Grieve Losses
Mascot	4) Identify Strengths of the Child

and	5) Learn to Appreciate the Child Inside
Lost Child:	6) Learn How to Integrate the Child Inside
	7) Learn to be Sensitive to the Child Inside

RELAPSE/PLATEAU

Enabler,	1) Learn Own Relapse Signs
Responsible	2) Learn Plateau Signs
Child,	3) Learn Behaviors that Maintain Relapse
Scapegoat,	
Mascot	4) Learn Behaviors that Maintain Plateau
and	
Lost Child:	5) Learn Behaviors that Stop Relapse
	6) Learn Behaviors that Stop Plateau

R

5

The Poppy Fields
(Relapse/Plateau Symptoms)

Dorothy and her friends were almost at the doorstep of Oz when they were tricked by the Wicked Witch's alluring sleep-inducing Poppy Fields. Even though they were so very close to their destination, Dorothy, Toto and the Cowardly Lion fell into a gentle sleep and were willing to delay their journey to take a short nap. The Tin Man and the Scarecrow pushed forward, while Glenda, the Good Witch, gave assistance to the sleeping trio and encouraged them to continue their quest.

So, too, is the journey for Adult Childen in the recovery process. In early recovery, progress is rapid and fulfilling but at times tricks of the Wicked Witch — the "Poppy Fields" — seem to appear. While some of us fall asleep during our recovery process, others are unaffected by the Poppy Fields just as the Tin Man and the Scarecrow. Not every Adult Child is caught "napping" in the same fashion as another. This chapter is a warning to be aware of the tricks which may lure you out of your recovery.

Awareness is the key. It is easier to face the journey if you know where you may encounter pitfalls in your recovery process. Sleeping or napping in the Poppy Fields are actually "relapse symptoms" or, in more specific terms, *plateaus* for Adult Children of Alcoholics. These plateaus can lure you into a permanent destruction of your forward movement. (The term *plateau* indicates no forward movement but CAN serve as a neutral resting place, while a *relapse* indicates regression, a backward movement.) A forewarned Adult Child can utilize this awareness wisely and move forward once again.

Just as Dorothy fought to find her way home, we too must bravely face the challenges of plateaus. Use the following information concerning plateaus (relapses) to your advantage — they are natural barriers.

Dorothy was aided by Glenda out of the devastating grasp of the Wicked Witch's trap. You, too, will be given the insight to move onward. No "crystal balls" are promised, but light will be shed on some good, solid skills to help you hold on to the Ruby Slippers that protect your journey home.

Please note: The reference to "coming home" indicates a journey into recovery which will elicit a feeling of being fully alive and discovering a wondrous, colorful new world. "Coming home" relates to the stage where there is love and belief in one's self.

In co-dependency, Melody Beattie notes that ACoAs believe that "The magic is in others, not in us . . . The good feelings are in them, not us . . . They have it all, we have nothing." This distorted thinking relates so well to the cast of characters in the Wizard of Oz, for everyone believed that it was the Wizard that had all the powers. The "coming home" was the realization of having their *own powers* and loving themselves. Our hope is to assist you in your journey to create *your own home within yourself!*

N

DEFINITIONS:

plateau: a period of leveling off in the stages of learning and development.

relapse: 1. to lapse back, as into disease after partial recovery; 2. to return to bad habits or ways; 3. to backslide.

> "I felt myself sliding back into my old patterns. I didn't even seem to care. I was backsliding so fast. It was as if I had never dealt with my issues, as if I wasn't on the road to recovery, I felt so bad. I was destroying myself so fast! How could that be after eight months of therapy? I was suicidal!? I was ready to kill myself? Wasn't I the survivor? Hadn't I felt so assured by my recovery program?"

The above is a common relapse incident as told by a recovering Adult Child of an Alcoholic client named Laura. Relapses and/or plateaus are scary phases for recovering alcoholics, co-dependents and Adult Children of Alcoholics who have been dealing with their core recovery issues. Some address the core issues of over-responsibility, while others address caretaking, people-pleasing or perfectionism. Core issues are as individual as each Adult Child.

The recovery process is a long hard painful program and then, just as it seems there is progress being made, almost out of the blue, a relapse occurs. Alcoholics go back to the bottle during a relapse; but more specifically, they go back to old alcoholic behaviors and patterns before the actual first drop of alcohol is taken (Gorski & Miller). Co-dependents relapse and, thereafter, return to enabling. Similarly, the Adult Child of an Alcoholic relapses into old destructive patterns.

The alcoholic has alcohol during his/her relapse; the Adult Child experiences extreme, intensified depression during this plateau/relapse recovery phase. Depression is the over-riding emotional response to the relapse stage. The following is an example of such a response, made by Dot, a remarkably intelligent and sensitive ACoA.

> *"At every step backward, I am ready to declare myself at square one again, if not further back. It is tough to hold on to any sense of enduring achievement. I feel forever doomed to wrestle with a fatalism that screams, 'You'll never change long enough to really make a difference in your life.' Sometimes I am so weary from it all that I just want to quit!"*

Every alcoholic is eternally fearful of a relapse, but a relapse for an Adult Child or co-dependent can *strengthen* a recovery process if the following occurs.

1. It is recognized as a plateau or relapse and not a *total loss* of all that has been accomplished. (It is imperative to note that *relapse* has a harsh, destructive connotation and what is actually happening to the Adult Child or co-dependent is a *plateauing* process. Relapse is a *repression of forward movement*.)
2. It is realized that this relapse is a *normal stage* of recovery.
3. The relapse is utilized as a *positive* "internal need" to deal with a *new* grief/loss issue.

The effects of the Poppy Field's sleep could have been destructive in Dorothy's journey to Oz. Likewise, the plateau stage, when denied or viewed as "fatal", can be detrimental to our personal recovery. We have the CHOICE to utilize this awareness to strengthen our potential for recovery.

BEHAVIORAL CHANGES LEADING TO RELAPSE

1. The Great and Powerful Oz (Reality Distortions)

The Wizard hid behind his thunderous voice and fiery mask — his control and power were merely a facade. The Wizard was actually a man hiding his pain. Dorothy and her friends experienced his distortions of their reality. Be cautious of distortions.

Reality distortion, a common and deeply-rooted core issue of Adult Children, manifests itself through years of intensive training and practice. As young children we may have stated "Oh, Dad's drinking isn't that bad, he's not an alcoholic." Perhaps we were the victims of our mother's violent physical abuse and responded with the intense message, "I *caused* Mom to beat me, I *did* make my bed wrong!" Or, as our teary-eyed mother walked into the living room after leaving the fight with our alcoholic father, we asked, "What's the matter, Mom?" our mother distorts reality and replied "Nothing!" We ignore (or distort) the reality of the situation, despite what we see with our eyes. We learned not to trust our own judgment — we learned to distort. An Adult Child's distorted reality is exemplified when stating (especially by the Mascot and some Responsible Children), "I haven't been affected by my alcoholic family of origin."

Hastings and Typpo's book, *An Elephant in the Living Room*, discusses a giant elephant that lives in our home — the one we walk around . . . carefully, so very carefully. We can escape the swinging, slapping trunk . . . sometimes. No one talks about the elephant, or what can be done with that giant destructive elephant in the home. There are certain rules about this pachyderm: we don't see it, we don't talk about it and certainly

A

we have no feelings about the huge elephant that has invaded our very existence. In reality, the elephant in the home is the alcoholic and we, the Adult Children, are still minimizing and distorting today's reality. Distortion can occur in the forms of (1) maximizing our unrealistic expectations of ourselves and others, and becoming overwhelmed with the issues; or (2) minimizing our abilities, our self-worth, our need to address issues at hand and our recovery successes.

Maximizing is a common form of relapse which focuses on the belief that "I can now fix it all — for myself and for everyone! I've got a recovery program now, I'm getting healthy and I can now fix everyone much better than before!!" (This will be further explained in the section concerning impatience with self due to expectations, *"You Could Scare The Crows In Kansas."*)

The minimizing concept is illustrated by Cindy, an adult Lost Child who binges and purges repeatedly to deal with reality and emotional starvation. She has difficulty accepting at gut level the seriousness of being an ACoA. Cindy remains in denial despite the obvious outward and inward self-destruction of her body and mind.

Minimizing is a very common step leading to a relapse. Another example of minimizing can be illustrated by the following example. After 24 weeks of intensive therapy, Cindy noted a plateau/relapse as she initiated the denial process and doubted that her father was alcoholic. She minimized once again the hold that alcohol had on her life.

Dorothy minimized her abilities. Her distortions did not allow her to believe in herself. The distortions of her inner strength were a destructive force in her journey home. If Dorothy had just believed in herself, instead of the Ruby Slippers or the Wizard, she would have made the trip "home" much sooner.

2. The Facade of the Wizard (Dishonesty With Self and Others)

The Wizard was dishonest with himself and all his subjects in Oz. He had everyone fooled into believing he had magical powers. For a while, his denial and dishonesty were so intense that he had almost fooled himself. The illusion created by the Wizard was extremely harmful to him and his kingdom — he became something he was not. He halted his own recovery and started to play games and manipulate others in his kingdom.

Dishonesty with self and others usually takes a form of rationalization. Rationalization is a process which intellectually makes sense of something that otherwise doesn't make sense. It is internal "deception functioning".

A client named Amy reported that she relapsed when she faced a new situation and she rationalized her intentions to benefit herself. Amy stated, "The thought of looking at the situation realistically is 'blacked out' because *I want to take control* and I must be dishonest and rationalize to do so." Amy had always been proud of her ability to be the perfect "game player" (just like the Wizard). In fact, Amy was ecstatic when she could out-game herself and others, but finally relapsed when she was confronted with her game-playing, manipulation and dishonesty.

Laura describes her dishonesty as "not admitting to myself or others how I really feel — that would be admitting weakness and a lack of control." Another group member, Rose, compares herself to a child who avoids the truth with the hope that "If I wait long enough, the problems will disappear."

Dishonesty takes other forms such as manipulations and power plays. We have become masters at power struggles, which were modeled in our homes of origin. Relationships are generally one-up, one-down in nature.

One person is the victor, the other is the loser. Adult Children find that they are dishonest with themselves and others to gain the one-up position. We find ourselves using bribes, threats, lies, manipulations and verbal, physical and mental abuse to win the distorted battle.

Sylvia reports that she uses sexuality as a means of dishonesty. She states, "I can make any man stay in love with me by doing anything he desires and faking my enjoyment." She has been fearful that if she is honest with her partner and herself, she will be abandoned. During therapy Sylvia realized her dishonesty and decided to deal with her own needs. This conclusion was prompted by a breakup with her partner, two weeks of depression and thoughts of suicide.

3. Only The Wizard Can Help (Sabotaging)

The Wicked Witch was dead; the courageous foursome had destroyed her evil rule. Despite this fact, Dorothy sabotaged her journey by once again not believing in her own powers. Idealistically she thought that only the Wizard and Glenda held the power to send her home. As a result of such thinking, she sabotaged the strength she had discovered in herself along the Yellow Brick Road.

Many times we sabotage our forward progress by creating a crisis to deal with others' concerns. We set up these crises so we can rescue victims, take control and thereby gain inner self-worth. By dealing with others' crises and externally fixing others, we can once again eliminate the need to deal with our own feelings and issues. If the focus is on others, then there is no progress in the recovery journey. (This is further explained in the section concerning the need to fix others/control, *"The Reign of The Wizard".*)

L

Sabotaging is a means of setting yourself up for a fall. Adult Children have difficulty with the calmness that comes when all is going well.

"In my childhood, things were calm only before the storm," reports Sue, "and I don't like not knowing what awful things will happen to me next." In group therapy Sue confided that she is extremely anxious whenever there is calmness in her recovery and sabotages her program in some fashion. "If things are going well with my husband, I find myself starting a fight just to break the calm. I'm scared of what will happen next, I guess."

As Adult Children we often fail to see the progress in our recovery. Sabotaging is enhanced by not keeping a daily inventory of recovery progress made in selected areas of focus. Without rewarding and praising ourselves for our accomplishments, we fall victims to the same sabotage that Dorothy experienced — the sabotaging of our own self-esteem and self-worth. Without daily evaluations, we have an excuse to go back to old, familiar habits and behaviors and their consequences. Ernie Larsen, in *Stage II, Recovery*, states that 98% of what we do is done out of habit. It is difficult to change that high percentage of self-destructive patterns without daily evaluations.

4. You Could Scare The Crows In Kansas (Impatience With Self Due to Expectations)

The Scarecrow began his journey to Oz to attain a brain, thinking that if he had a brain he would be clever enough to scare crows. Dorothy told the Scarecrow that he had the brains to scare all the crows in Kansas, but the Scarecrow dismissed Dorothy's claim. At the end of his journey, he realized that he had the intelligence he sought all along, just as Dorothy had said. The realization of his powers was discovered when he was patient and loving with himself.

Impatience with yourself and others can cause your program to plateau indefinitely!

As Adult Children we have exceedingly high expectations of ourselves and others in our lives. It appears that impatience with self is not limited to just the Responsible Child. ACoAs have been little adults almost since birth and have learned to have unrealistically high expectations. We have had to be mothers, cooks, clowns, pleasurers, caretakers and award-winners to gain worth. Self-esteem, what little there is, was not gained by attempting to meet our own expectations, but by attempting to meet other people's expectations. Distorted expectations of self are generally noted in Adult Children.

In lectures, Claudia Black speaks of ACoAs who think they can move mountains — and if by some chance they do, they expect us to be out there waiting to applaud. Nothing is ever good enough or done well enough for many Adult Children. This distortion of abilities can only lead to repeated failures, low self-esteem and relapse.

Not only do we relapse because of high expectations of ourselves, but many times we increase our failure rate by setting further limitations, particularly by allowing short allotments of time and having unrealistic expectations for personal success.

One client remarked, "Not only do I continue to have unrealistically high goals set for myself but I apply short amounts of allowable time in which to attain them. In one year how can I expect to be a 'master of techniques learned' to correct the survival skills of an entire lifetime? It's hard for me to acknowledge a positive success as being worth anything, or to allow myself time to learn and make mistakes in the process."

Many Adult Children also expect others to mind-read, a practice that we unwittingly use with great consistency. In an alcoholic home we learn to mind-read family members to escape trauma, broken promises, abuse and criticism. We assume the thoughts of teachers, friends and relatives. In fact, many times we learn to distort reality so that our mind-reading becomes accurate. Adult Children believe that if *we* are expected to read the minds of others, then *others* must be able to read our minds and know what *we* need and want.

An ACoA named Brenda stated, "Friends should read my mind and know what I expect because *I* know what *they* need." Brenda has set up a pattern of people-pleasing and unrealistic expectations of her friends' and her own abilities. Gladys, a fellow group member, further complicates the issue by stating, "People should read my mind and know how I'm feeling and react accordingly."

When we have unrealistic expectations of ourselves and others, the result is generally a setup for failure. Clients in therapy state the following: "Why should life be so hard for me?"; "Haven't I paid a large enough price in my life for Dad's alcoholism?"; "Why can't I be healthy now?" These "self-talk tapes" (repetitive tapes that are internal) are examples of self-pity or the "poor ol' me" syndrome. Self-pity is surely on the teetering edge of relapse and the cause of setting unrealistic expectations on others and self.

5. You Had To Learn It For Yourself (Getting Facts Only)

Although Glenda told Dorothy about the powers she held within, Dorothy believed that her shoes held the power. During her final moments in Oz, Dorothy realized the truth: She had all she needed within herself. Glenda again assured Dorothy that she had had it all along, and just needed to admit that to return home to Kansas.

Many Adult Children enter therapy or an ACoA group as if the concept is to "get it and go". In many instances we want everything we can get our hands on concerning Adult Children and core issues. Constantly wanting more, we grab book after book. "Oh, a Claudia Black book — great!" "A book by Woititz — good! Got any more?" "Oh, a new one by Wegscheider-Cruse — terrific!" We eat the books up, but never take the time to *really digest* the information and integrate it into our lives. The facts are taken in, but not the skills to make our lives more meaningful and beautiful. What good is all this newly-found knowledge if it isn't used?

Relapse is always lurking around the corner. Gravitz and Bowden in *A Guide To Recovery* talk of the five-step approach to recovery. Both believe it's not just attaining the educational information that elicits recovery, it's the *complete process of integration of that information into a new, healthy life.* Integration takes time, work, acceptance of grief and loss and examination of personal pain.

On the opposite side of the spectrum, some of us experience a different phenomenon — we don't want the facts. The facts mean reality, and reality leads to pain. Stirring the pot brings the garbage to the top. Many of us remark, "If we see the facts, we will have to deal with the emotions and create a change." That process involves risks, uncertainty, and grieving. This type of thinking surely leads to a long nap in the Poppy Fields.

6. Miss Gulch Can't Get Us! (Escape/Fantasy)

Dorothy grabs Toto and runs away . . . far, far away to escape the terrifying Miss Gulch. Dorothy tells Professor Marvel in the forest that she will accompany him to see the Seven Wonders of the World. This is a means of escaping the clutches of Miss Gulch. Dorothy believes that an escape is the only way to keep Toto away from Miss Gulch.

Escaping is a very common behavioral change leading to a relapse. Escaping can occur in one of two conditions: (1) when a new issue has been recognized and must be dealt with in therapy; (2) an issue that an Adult Child is attempting to face without dealing with the loss or grief necessary to work through the issue. Generally, when we think of escape we think of the Lost Child role, although many other Adult Children utilize this behavior during relapse.

Lynette, a Responsible Child in therapy, tells of sleeping binges of 12-14 hours during an escape phase. She states, "It's responsible to sleep. I'm a workaholic, and *this* escape is acceptable."

Many ACoAs use food as an escape. Sandy, who was a Lost Child in her home of origin, has utilized food as an escape for over 30 years. The escape of binging and purging is set in motion when Sandy doesn't face an issue and confront her feelings. Escaping with food tends to be common with Adult Children who many times have some form of eating disorder (overeating, bulimia or anorexia). Food is used as an escape to gain personal emotional nurturing.

After 30 weeks of group therapy dealing with core issues, the members of an ACoA group noted that they began binging. After the meeting, one generally quiet client named Kris remarked she had been overeating after the last three sessions. With investigation, the group realized that the topic for the past three weeks had been "anger" and all the members had been dealing openly with their issues during the sessions and then "stuffing" the feelings back down with food when they returned home.

Diane and Barb escape family conflict and retreat into relapse by allowing themselves to be consumed with books. Books, in this instance, serve as an escape and/or fantasy from family communication and dealing with issues at hand. Laura states that she hides in her room when she is depressed and never wants to come out.

Upon examination, we find many habits learned in our families of origin for survival are still used by us as adults as a form of escape during a relapse.

A client named Rose states that she uses the *Scarlett O'Hara escape:* "It will be all better tomorrow." This escape is common with Adult Children. In Rose's home of origin it was always a pattern of extreme ups and downs. She learned as a child that things generally were better the day after. If her dad came home and verbally abused the entire family, it appeared that all was forgotten the next day. Rose learned not to talk about what happened the night before. It almost seemed as though it never really happened (reality distortion). The reality of the situation was dismissed by everyone and the escape from reality was a common family occurrence.

7. The Reign Of The Wizard (Need to "Fix" Others/Control)

The Wizard feels his purpose is to fix others. His "fixing" takes the form of hiding behind his smoke, fire and mask, and then gaining praise for his work. He also manifests control of his subjects by causing them to believe he is the only one who can fix any problem that occurs. He is the "Great and Powerful Oz". The hiding keeps the Wizard from facing his own vulnerabilities and the fact that he is, in reality, a carnival balloonist from Omaha — not a magical Wizard.

Many of us note relapse symptoms when we fall back into the old patterns of needing to "fix" others. The payoffs for fixing behaviors have been positive strokes and illusions of increased self-esteem and self-worth. We as ACoAs miss the feelings of importance gained from others and the deeply gratifying feelings of being needed.

When we experience the early stages of relapse with fixing behaviors, we tend to lose sight of our own needs.

Z

Anger and resentment are the result. Many of us can relate this facet of relapse to our intense struggle with over-responsibility and the need to be in control of all situations. This is especially true when we experience the haunting memories of childhood which were so "out of control". As ACoAs we decide in childhood that we will always be in control when we grow up. The distortion is formulated: "If I have control, no tornados (like the tornado in Kansas) will rip through my life like they did when I was a child."

Amy relates that she feels responsible for those who are dealing with the issues she has already addressed in therapy. She feels it is *her responsibility* to show others her path of recovery. The belief was that her journey was the only path to "Oz". She is now coming to realize she was not fixed by the magic of others — she had to work on her own issues at her own rate and readiness. Amy has admitted this is her biggest struggle in her role as a Responsible Child. Her home of origin dictated that she tell others to "do this or do that". She states that she really believed she could fix everyone and it was only *she* who could do the fixing.

Another facet of the "need to fix relapse" is the inability to say "no". This can be especially true of people newly involved in the recovery process. Dot struggled with the difficulty of saying "no" to fixing others and she oftentimes fell back into "stuffing". The guilt of not "fixing" her recovery/support family had been a source of plateauing/relapse in Dot's recovery. The pattern was complicated by the fear of rejection, usually to an unreasonable degree, which accompanied a refusal to do something for another. Many times we slip into a relapse triggered by another old familiar (pre-recovery) response. All too soon we feel trapped like a hamster who runs on and on and on in an endless wire wheel. When Dot became aware of her own needs and the necessity of selectively saying "no", she reclaimed her self and her right to recovery.

8. No Time For Tomorrow (Not Dealing with Own Issues Anymore)

Dorothy and her friends rush to get to the Land of Oz. They believe the sooner they finish their journey, the sooner they will gain their reward. However, the reward is to be found within themselves all along. The characters run so fast down the Yellow Brick Road that they do not see the growth they have made along the way. The Tin Man had always been caring and kind. The Lion had always been brave in the face of danger. The Scarecrow had always had brilliant ideas. The difficult journey might have been easier if they had known to look within themselves.

In late-to-middle stages of recovery, many ACoAs feel as though they just *can't* deal with one more core issue. Some have noted they get to a stage where they say "enough of all this" and want to discontinue therapy. This is especially true with clients who have been in therapy for over six months. Clients forget the progress they have made in the past months and start to numb themselves to new issues they *know* must be addressed. Just confronting the issue of needing to go on may be a motivation to eliminate the relapse. Once we allow ourselves a short rest and time to think, we can work through a minor plateau. The key is the early awareness of what is going on within. It also means allowing ourselves the liberty to do what is necessary to recover, instead of smothering ourselves with unrealistic expectation full of self-accusing "shoulds". We need to stop "shoulding" on ourself!

We believe that many of our Adult Children who are at advanced stages of therapy have not allowed themselves a "resting period" after significant, quick recovery in past months. These clients do not realize that everyone needs a "shutdown time" to settle after growth. As mentioned earlier in the *Six Steps for ACoAs*, (Chapter 2 —

"Leaving the Black and White World Behind"), many Adult Children cannot justify a real vacation but can warrant giving themselves a mental vacation. This can result in numbness or depression. On various occasions the shutdown or mental vacation is the step before facing a big issue which generally involves anger, grief or loss.

Jan began her relapse by going back to old destructive behaviors. She started to "fix" others, once again giving up control to others and becoming a people-pleaser. She stuffed her feelings emotionally and shoved those feelings even further down with compulsive spending patterns of buying presents for others.

When Jan confronted the real core issue, she realized that she was not dealing with the grief and loss of the death of her grandmother. Actually, Jan had felt responsible for her grandmother's death because she was the only person in the room when her grandmother died. Jan had not allowed herself to grieve, and in her mind she became solely responsible for the death. To compensate, Jan had stuffed her grief to avoid the fear of pain. Jan had refused to look at the situation from a realistic viewpoint, and for nine years had allowed distorted thinking to entrap her in feelings of shame and guilt. She had been stuffing her feelings and trying to please those who were alive to appease her inner guilt and shame. Once confronted with the need to face her loss and grief, Jan accepted that she was not responsible for her grandmother's death, thereby allowing herself to recapture the love that she felt for her grandmother. Jan, now working through her death issues, realizes that she was at a plateau stage.

Dot responded in a similar fashion when she stated that she could not go on with therapy. She admitted that she was "tired of all this work, always finding more to address — it is so hopeless!" As she looked at the floor, she admitted to the group that she was fearful of her own being and discussed her traumatic emotional breakdown many years ago. Dot was terrified because

A

she had found herself in a minor depression for weeks, unable to accomplish tasks at work, unable to have healthy relationships with her family, and found that she had pulled emotionally and physically away from her husband.

During an exercise on "needs assessment attainments", she came to the realization that she had unmet needs from her childhood. Upon closer examination, she realized that she had not fully addressed her loss and grief issues with her alcoholic father who was emotionally and physically unavailable to her as a child. She became aware that she had tried to attain those unmet childhood needs with every man in her life. Dot came to the conclusion that she was a compulsive lover (patterns of destructive loving) and was addicted to relationships to fill her void of abandonment by her father.

As discussed in an earlier chapter, many times we deal with the issues of other people in an attempt to avoid our own issues. Sue stated, "I look for a victim whom I can rescue, and then I won't have to look at me for a while." She also found that her issues surrounded compulsive loving patterns. Historically, Sue's father had emotionally and physically abandoned her as a child while he was in the late stages of alcoholism. She looked for someone to rescue over and over again, and fulfilled her unmet needs with lovers and husbands. Both Dot and Sue had tried to repress their needs to deal with those unmet needs through compulsive loving. Each had found their own way of escaping the painful exploration of the next core issue in their recovery process.

9. The Horse Of A Different Color (External Referencing)

Dorothy and company circle the doorstep of the Emerald City, watching the Horse of a Different Color change from yellow to green to blue right before their eyes. All stare in amazement as they watch their reality alter and question what they have just experienced.

During early phases of recovery, we learn to refocus our energies from "others" to "selves". This external referencing had in the past become a source of praise, self-worth and self-esteem. A client named Jan reported that she was always doing too much — making treats for school holidays for all her childrens' classmates, making special Friday gourmet meals to please her family, helping friends with their personal problems, as well as chairing *five* community committees. Jan, looking quite pale, spoke of her physical and emotional exhaustion. She stated she had repeatedly pushed herself past her limit. When questioned about this, she replied, "But everyone needs me and they all think I'm great!" Jan's source of worth was external — it came from other's praise.

During "refocusing", the recovering Adult Child learns skills to gain internal referencing through internal praise, strokes, approval and acceptance of self-worth. The pattern is difficult to change, but progress is generally noted within one to two months of therapy. Most of us find some inner confidence and self-worth, while building up our personal approval skills, as the need for external referencing decreases sharply. During a relapse, however, there tends to be a gradual increase in the need for external referencing. The insidious decay of internal referencing once again gives way to the need for others' approval.

Laura, after one year of therapy, relapsed by increasing her need to fix others as she had in the past. She reported that she felt her progress in therapy was not as dramatic as in the past months (she had not kept up her daily journal and daily inventory of accomplishments) and needed to help others in order to feel worthy again. It was almost like getting a "dose of speed" — that rush of being great and being needed!!!

External referencing can be addictive in nature. The "high" gained is quickly lost, almost like the effects of cocaine. The destructive cost to oneself is great in comparison to the effects received.

Many of us change our colors to fit any circumstance and any person. Relapse occurs when we alter our behaviors to change for others to gain worth. This "Poppy Field" is very subliminal in nature. Be cautious — external referencing is a tricky witch.

Examples of Areas Noted in Relapse

1. Getting worth from spouse's accomplishments (raise, job, advancement, honors).

2. Gaining worth from children's accomplishments (home run at baseball game, role in a school play).

3. Searching out dysfunctional people to "fix" for the praise gained (friends, co-workers, volunteer work).

4. Concentrating on the problems of other people and seeking solutions for their worries and concerns, thus taking focus off your own program.

5. Repeatedly starting new projects to gain approval but never finishing the projects which were begun.

6. Eliciting and manipulating approval from others to validate self-esteem.

7. Gaining self-worth from spouse's comments, compliments, while losing sight of inner power.

In relapse we may strive to attain external praise, and once again internalize negatives given by others. Sandy, a Responsible Child and Mascot, noted her relapse when she once again began to want strokes and praise from her alcoholic mother. "I knew she wouldn't give me what I needed, and I knew she'd minimize whatever I

T

did," Sandy sobbed as she spoke of her own sabotaging of progress. "I've worked so hard to detach from my mom's negative remarks, and once again I set myself up for pain." Of all the relapse symptoms, external referencing is the most obvious clue to a relapse phase.

During recovery, our "inner child" surfaces and we give ourselves nurturing. We begin to love, care for and nurture ourselves in a healthy manner. Whenever the recovering "child within" is put on hold for others' approval, progress is halted.

10. Surrender Dorothy (Increased Usage of Cross-Addictions)

Entrapped within the castle, Dorothy feels hopeless and helpless. Her inner strength is not enough to make her feel secure. In fact, she is utterly terrified. She surrenders and tells the Witch to take her ruby slippers. Dorothy is ready to use any means to flee from the Witch's clutches.

During the early stages of a plateau, many Adult Children have found that they turn with increasing frequency to various cross-addictions. Cross-addictions may take the form of eating disorders (bulimia, anorexia or overeating), overspending, over-responsibility, workaholism, gambling, addictive loving, substance abuse, etc.

When Cindy, a Lost Child, is near a relapse, she increases her people-pleasing efforts and stuffs feelings once again. Guilt, shame and pain surface and Cindy stuffs those uncomfortable emotions down with binging. After the binge the shame is intensified and emotions run rampant. The purging phase of the cycle then begins with the abuse of laxatives and vomiting. Shame, guilt and pain encompass the purge and the cycle continues over and over again.

Rick reports when feelings of resentment and anger were stirring, he would buy things for himself and his family to compensate. Rick relapsed after 16 weeks of therapy. He realized that his alcoholic father had not met his needs as a child, which left Rick angry. His father was always distant, cold and proved his competence to the world with his wealth. But Rick had been unwilling to address his anger about those things. Instead, he followed his father's pattern by trying to fill his unmet needs with inanimate "things" in his life.

Rick discovered that he could only be a "success" if he had "things" to show his worth. With an accumulation of "things" Rick thought that he could gain his dad's acceptance, as well as the love of his wife and child. Finally Rick worked through the relapse and addressed his issues of abandonment, unmet childhood needs, grief and loss. He later also had to address his compulsive spending and his $15,000 accumulated debt.

Sharon revealed during a relapse she had once again fallen back into old destructive behaviors. Investigation of her destructive patterns included indulging in an abuse of "speed", marijuana and alcohol. Sharon concluded that she had been avoiding her issues of enabling her boyfriend and denying his alcoholism.

Cross-addictions are powerful tools that are utilized for nurturing of self in early phases of relapse. Patrick Carnes, in his book, *The Sexual Addiction*, illustrated a cyclical pattern by correlating alcoholism to sexual addiction. A similar cycle can be illustrated when dealing with Adult Children and their cross-addictions.

In Figure 4.1, an Adult Child begins the cycle with a *faulty belief system* which is learned in the dysfunctional home of origin. Beliefs include old messages like, "I'm not lovable; I'm not good," "It's all my fault" and "I'm not capable." These beliefs lead to *distorted thinking*. As our thinking is distorted, we begin to exhibit our ACoA core characteristics (people-pleasing, approval-seeking, over-responsibility, fear of authority, etc.) and our feelings become *unmanageable*. The feelings are not dealt with and the vicious cycle continues. The process may be similar to the following examples.

Figure 4.1. Cross-Addictive Cycle.

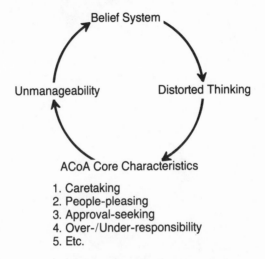

1. Caretaking
2. People-pleasing
3. Approval-seeking
4. Over-/Under-responsibility
5. Etc.

John goes to work and finds he has a note on his desk instructing him to see his supervisor. Immediately, his old message *(faulty belief system)* channels a thought to his mind: "You've had it now. You're in trouble." *Distorted thinking* increases the vicious cycle as he inches toward the supervisor's door. He concludes, "I know I messed up that financial report yesterday. I always screw it up. I can never do anything right — it's hopeless." This impaired thinking kicks in the ACoA *core characteristics* of fear of authority figures and criticism. The plot thickens as he nears the door. "I know he'll fire me. I'll have to leave town. I'll be so humiliated by it all. What will my wife say when I tell her I've lost my job? He'll yell for an hour after this goof-up." John's belief system further shouts, "You'll always be a failure. Give it up. End all of this now." The cycle continues until John enters the supervisor's door or addresses his issues. (The irony is the supervisor may be wanting to praise him.)

Sometimes, however, the pattern changes (Figure 4.2a). Say, for instance, the same situation occurs, but this time when John gets to his *distorted thinking* and fear of criticism, he uses something he has always used to

Figure 4.2. Cross-Addictive Cycles.

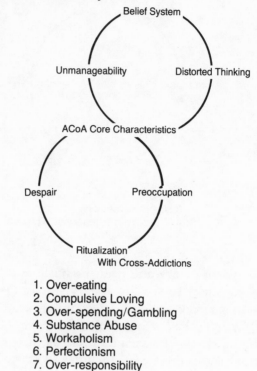

1. Over-eating
2. Compulsive Loving
3. Over-spending/Gambling
4. Substance Abuse
5. Workaholism
6. Perfectionism
7. Over-responsibility

escape his feelings — workaholism *(his cross-addiction)*.
John decides he must return to his compulsive pattern of
over-responsibility. The *ritual* for John is compensating
by working longer and longer hours. John feels he is
giving up his personal needs to compensate by overpro-
ducing. "If I work all day and until 10:00 tonight, I know
I can redo that report."

John initiates the *ritual* of breaking promises with his
wife and children for tonight — a basketball game and
pizza. John feels the despair of letting his family down.
He feels the *despair* in realizing that he once again has
gone back to his old behaviors of workaholism. He
remembers that his wife swore she'd divorce him if this
preoccupation with work continued. But he has no choice!
He will lose his self-respect unless he "proves himself!"

The cycle continues until a point of crisis for John (and his family).

Oftentimes as ACoAs we maintain ourselves in Figure 4.2 and only utilize our cross-addictions. As previously noted, during plateauing cross-addictions increase dramatically. The cross-addictions can become powerful, destructive forces which lead to relapse and depression.

Remember Dorothy's trip into the beautiful Poppy Fields? The Witch's voice in the background shrieked . . . the flowers were so beautiful but they were also poisonous. The Wicked Witch lured, "The poppies, the poppies . . ."

11. Time's Running Out (Overwhelmed Once Again)

The red particles of sand are trickling down through the hourglass. Dorothy's captured state is overwhelming as she is alone, frightened and rapidly running out of time. As each particle sifts through the hourglass, Dorothy became increasingly overwhelmed by her inevitable fate of doom. Dorothy sits crying and sobbing in her castle prison, unable to attempt an escape for herself.

Many of us find ourselves as horrified and overwhelmed as Dorothy was in her castle prison. Sue recalls sobbing in a session as she once again felt caught in quicksand. Sue made the analogy that she felt like she couldn't grasp anything to stop her decline. "It's all so hopeless!"

In early recovery we are given the awareness of the facts that are needed for recovery to begin. Just as Glenda the Good Witch guided Dorothy, recovering Adult Children need to be guided through one issue at a time. The reason is clear — to keep the program simple and workable. Focusing on a single goal helps us from feeling overwhelmed.

Ann recollects having grown so much in therapy. Group members had watched her bloom into a beautiful butterfly willing to soar to meet new risks and challenges. She was willing to address the biggest risk in her recovery phase — a decision concerning her marriage to an alcoholic spouse.

Meticulously, she planned the steps in her decision for separation. She would not fail if she took sufficient time to examine all of the choices. Through the integration of skills learned in therapy, Ann became strong and insightful. But what Ann had not planned on was her husband's sobriety and inpatient treatment.

Unfortunately, she gave up her own recovery program and allowed herself to center her life around her husband's new sobriety program. Bill, her husband, relapsed after one week out of the treatment facility, and Ann fell apart. She had given up the pursuit of her own recovery and had spent the last month working on Bill. Ann was devastated and overwhelmed. Eventually she confronted her own behavior and swore to never again lose sight of the power she held within herself. Never again would she become so overwhelmed and helpless!

Unfortunately, some relapses can be life-threatening. Hillary, a sensitive Lost Child, reports that she attempted suicide while feeling overwhelmed with her inability to control her boyfriend. She believed she had taken every path to "capture" her Prince Charming. Hillary lived in a world of fantasy. Her overwhelmingly distorted plan was to capture her love by attempting suicide and then have her Prince save her at the last moment. Fortunately, she found the strength to save her own life and called a friend, who took her to the emergency room. After months of intensive inpatient and outpatient therapy she regained — *the love of herself!*

Today Hillary has developed awareness of the Poppy Fields and has learned to address her warning signs before allowing herself to become overwhelmed once again.

12. We'll Never Save Dorothy (Focus on the Negatives)

The Lion, Tin Man, Scarecrow and Dorothy cautiously walk down the long hall that houses the magical Wizard. They are within minutes of gaining their desires but the Cowardly Lion focuses on negatives. Fear begins to overwhelm him. Shaking, the Lion confesses that he won't have the courage to ask for courage when he finally meets the Wizard. The fear becomes so intense that the Lion sabotages himself. Pulling his own tail, the poor creature thinks that someone is behind him.

Marge remembers having screamed in pain, "I'm never going to be healthy! I'll never feel strong enough to leave this therapy group!" Marge, like many other Adult Children, quickly forgot her perilous path down the Yellow Brick Road. She forgot all the times she had already faced the "Wicked Witch" and gained progress, bringing herself closer to home.

Two of the most common plateau/relapse signs emerge when we (1) focus on our own negatives; and (2) when we look at what we still have not addressed in therapy. Marge's philosophy was, "Look how far I have to go," instead of, "Look how far I have come."

Gladys reiterates that she was nearly at a relapse when she realized a process that would aid her in her journey home. Her insight into relapse can be of great benefit to us all. The following *relapse work sheet* is a realistic approach to addressing the effects of "napping" (plateauing) in our recovery.

Relapse Worksheet

Ideally, the following chart should be used DAILY to keep track of accomplishments and daily concerns that need attention. (Please feel free to make additional copies for daily use.) The relapse sheet could be utilized as a problem-solving method in the early stages of plateauing, but it is designed to be used daily for maximum effectiveness.

The top section indicates the 6 (six) warning signs which can indicate the early signs of an impending plateau or relapse. Heed these warnings and you may avert a long sleep in the Poppy Fields.

Warning Signs

PHYSICAL SIGNS	EMOTIONAL SIGNS	LACK OF DECISION-MAKING
backaches, migraines, pain, stomach aches	depression, anger, rage, resentment	confusion, inability to initiate action
ISOLATION	**OVER-REACTING**	**DESTRUCTIVE HABITS**
physical, emotional escape, fantasy, sleep	over-sensitivity, blaming	drug/alcohol abuse overeating, over-spending

COLUMN 1	COLUMN 2	COLUMN 3	COLUMN 4
LOSS OF PROGRAM	WHERE AM I?	WHERE DO I WANT TO GO?	PLAN OF ACTION
old destructive behaviors: RELAPSE SIGNS	WHAT am I doing? HOW am I doing it? WHEN am I doing it? WHO am I doing it with?	WHAT have I done? HOW did I do it? WHEN did I do it? WHO did I do it with?	WHAT can I do? HOW can I do it? WHEN can I do it? WHO can help?
LOOK FOR:	ASK:	ASK:	ASK:
reality distortion	WHAT	WHAT	WHAT
	HOW	HOW	HOW
	WHEN	WHEN	WHEN
	WHO	WHO	WHO
dishonesty with self	WHAT	WHAT	WHAT
	HOW	HOW	HOW
	WHEN	WHEN	WHEN
	WHO	WHO	WHO
sabotaging	WHAT	WHAT	WHAT
	HOW	HOW	HOW
	WHEN	WHEN	WHEN
	WHO	WHO	WHO
impatience with self due to expectations	WHAT	WHAT	WHAT
	HOW	HOW	HOW
	WHEN	WHEN	WHEN
	WHO	WHO	WHO
getting facts only	WHAT	WHAT	WHAT
	HOW	HOW	HOW
	WHEN	WHEN	WHEN
	WHO	WHO	WHO

N

escape, fantasy	WHAT	WHAT	WHAT
	HOW	HOW	HOW
	WHEN	WHEN	WHEN
	WHO	WHO	WHO
need to fix others/control	WHAT	WHAT	WHAT
	HOW	HOW	HOW
	WHEN	WHEN	WHEN
	WHO	WHO	WHO
not dealing with own issues	WHAT	WHAT	WHAT
	HOW	HOW	HOW
	WHEN	WHEN	WHEN
	WHO	WHO	WHO
external referencing	WHAT	WHAT	WHAT
	HOW	HOW	HOW
	WHEN	WHEN	WHEN
	WHO	WHO	WHO
increase in cross-addictions	WHAT	WHAT	WHAT
	HOW	HOW	HOW
	WHEN	WHEN	WHEN
	WHO	WHO	WHO
overwhelmed once again	WHAT	WHAT	WHAT
	HOW	HOW	HOW
	WHEN	WHEN	WHEN
	WHO	WHO	WHO
focus on negatives	WHAT	WHAT	WHAT
	HOW	HOW	HOW
	WHEN	WHEN	WHEN
	WHO	WHO	WHO

unrealistic fears, resurface of fears	WHAT	WHAT	WHAT
	HOW	HOW	HOW
	WHEN	WHEN	WHEN
	WHO	WHO	WHO

Focus on the bottom section of the worksheet. The left column indicates the relapse/plateau symptoms (column 1) to be addressed in your recovery program.

Column 2, WHERE AM I?, indicates what you are seeing in yourself today. Ask yourself the four questions: WHAT? HOW? WHEN? and WHO? You may find that you have multiple signs indicated from column 1 and need to address each and every relapse issue that appears to be relevant to you today. This is a good mechanism to help you keep aware of where you are in your daily program.

Column 3 is a list of PAST ACCOMPLISHMENTS to utilize in your recovery. It is a column of things, that you have already used that work! Too often we find that we have forgotten our accomplishments. Column 3 focuses on SUCCESSES IN THE PAST to use as guides.

Many of us find ourselves moving backward! It is imperative that we retrace our steps of recovery to utilize our successes. You have to find WHAT WORKS FOR YOU!!! Column 3 will be your guide and a place to add your new accomplishments and sort out your mistakes. (Yes, ACoAs do make mistakes; it is part of a healthy, human recovery!)

Column 4 is a "plan of action" column. Use your imagination and brainstorm ideas to attain the outcome you desire. Remember, the key is in CHOICE. You have the ability to make choices and journey "home".

13. Lions and Tigers and Bears — Oh My! (Unrealistic Fears/ Fears Resurface)

The forest becomes dark and filled with strange noises, which frighten the trio. The group fears meeting animals, especially lions and tigers and bears. As they move forward they increase each other's fears by chanting, "Lions . . . and tigers . . . and bears . . . Oh my!" Their mutual obsession causes the three to become overwhelmed with fear.

Barb remembers when the holidays were nearing. This was the first time she would face her alcoholic home of origin since beginning therapy. She had struggled, grieved, and successfully progressed in therapy, but soon would come the day of reckoning. Barb had planned, practiced and visualized how she would react with her family of origin during this critical holiday time. She swore she would not return to her childhood Scapegoat role. She affirmed her wellness to herself as she neared the door of her parents' home.

The pressure began almost immediately. She was designated the black sheep of the family within hours of her arrival. Her siblings once again were much smarter, wiser, more competent and accepted. Despite all her planning, Barb quickly relapsed into old behaviors. She resumed her family Scapegoat role.

The preceding is a common incident reported by Adult Children. Fears resurface, become overwhelming and then take over our progress.

Bob, a handsome, capable man, had been in therapy for six months. He found that his fears constantly resurfaced and threatened to destroy his progress. Bob fantasized that one day he would go to his workplace and "they" would all find out . . . that he was incompetent! Bob was successful in the stressful workplace of a large, nationwide corporation. His competence was denied by no one but himself: "I fear they will find out I'm a failure," he confessed in therapy. "I've always been a failure — ever since I was little." Bob's childhood messages haunted his current life and his fears constantly embroiled his successful profession.

Bob is an example of an Adult Child whose fragile recovery is threatened by impending relapse. Bob and so many others feel the hopelessness that leads to relapse.

Once again we see the impending sleep in the poppy fields. Fear is such a powerful instigator during relapse. Addressing the fear and finding the power within is the only remedy in the journey home.

Conclusion

The Poppy Fields are filled with alluring traps to halt your recovery. Now you have the awareness of their existence. BUT THAT IS NOT ENOUGH! Remember, the awareness of an impending relapse can be aided by realizing the relapse or plateau symptoms and then addressing changes that need to occur.

As we reported in the beginning of the chapter: A relapse can strengthen your progress if (1) it is *realized as a plateau or relapse;* (2) it is realized that this relapse is a *normal stage* of recovery; (3) the relapse is understood as a *positive* "internal need" to re-evaluate progress and (4) the relapse is utilized as a positive internal need to deal with a new grief/loss issue.

You have the awareness. You know it is a normal stage. You know you must re-evaluate . . . but then what? Utilize the following process to aid your recovery. This problem-solving addressing method will aid your journey through the issue at hand.

Plateau Problem-Solving Methodology

(*See page 180 for full format*)

For an illustration, let's use Jan's (Section 8, *no time for tomorrow*) example of reaching a plateau because of evading a confrontation with the grief of her grandmother's death. As you remember, Jan had blamed herself for her grandmother's death because she had been the only person in the room at the moment it occurred. After eight years, she still retained internal blame. "Perhaps I should have given her a drink of water. I should have known. I should have called my dad, that would have helped," she sobbed. The grief had not been fully addressed.

Let's look at the first step. List issues as specifically as possible. Brainstorm to come up with ideas about what issue may be the cause of relapse. Don't be afraid to guess, and list as many ideas as possible (column 1).

Column 1	ISSUES TO BE ADDRESSED
1. Anger at not saying "no" to my father's request to buy presents for family	
2. Blaming myself for death of Grandma and retaining guilt	
3. Anger at myself for binging	
4. Sexual issues and dating	

Jan decides that the issue that is precipitating the pain is the grief of her grandmother's death (target top issue, column 2). She believes her inability to forgive herself has maintained a destructive pattern of people-pleasing. Jan has been "buying off" her family for years through approval-seeking devices such as good deeds, presents and compliments because she "took Grandma away from the family." She realizes she had lost herself within her family unit and was the one who made everyone happy — the pleaser. This has been ongoing at Jan's expense.

Column 2	TARGET TOP ISSUE
1. Death of Grandma (guilt/shame)	

Next we look at the old patterns of dealing with issues of guilt and shame: (column 3).

Column 3	OLD PATTERNS OF BEHAVIOR
1. Buy expensive presents for all siblings and parents for birthdays	
2. Buy nieces and nephews whatever they desired	
3. Conform to father's wishes	
4. Conform to mother's wishes	
5. Be at the family's beckoning call for any errand needed	
6. Lead life as parents and others desire	

Next look at how this was self destructive to Jan (column 4).

Column 4	HOW DESTRUCTIVE TO ME
1. Use food to stuff down feelings	
2. Financial debt through loans taken out from credit union	
3. Anxiety and panic whenever mother left town (fear of abandonment)	
4. Agoraphobia/panic attacks on an increasing basis	
5. Bulimia	
6. No time for self	
7. Feeling used by others	
8. Low self-esteem	
9. Anger, resentment of others	
10. Anger, resentment of self	

The next step is an important link in the problem-solving methodology (the old messages, column 5). Old messages help you understand the unmet childhood needs you continue to search out through life. Jan needed to be lovable, capable and successful in her family's eyes. Furthermore, she believed she was solely responsible for their happiness. In column 5, list what you believe were your old messages.

Column 5 OLD MESSAGES
1. I am not lovable. 2. I am not capable. 3. I am a failure. 4. It's ALL my fault.

The new messages set up powerful signals to change the "old tapes" which are distorted, mental killers inside us all. Jan's new messages were identified as the following:

Column 6 NEW MESSAGES
1. I **am** lovable. 2. I **am** capable in what I do. 3. I am **NOT** responsible for Grandma's death. 4. I **am** a success in my life. 5. I believe in the power **within** myself.

The next step is to identify means of working through the issue at hand. Brainstorm ideas (don't worry if you think they are silly ideas) that can be utilized to address the issue. Note Jan's ideas:

Column 7	BRAINSTORMING

1. Individual therapy to deal with grief and loss issues
2. Write a good-bye letter to Grandma
3. Visit Grandma's grave
4. Write letter of forgiveness to myself
5. Join OA (Overeaters Anonymous group) and eating-disorders therapy group
6. Accept my grief as a natural phase
7. Attend ACAnon group (ACoA self-help group)
8. Do my new message affirmations daily
9. Pray/meditate
10. Set up family meeting to discuss feelings concerning the death
11. Do volunteer work in a nursing home
12. Work in death/grief/loss workbook

The next step is a plan of action. Eliminate the ideas that are not needed or desired in your brainstorming (column 7). Remember, brainstorming is a means of gathering ideas. The ideas can be silly and later discarded, but they are options for evaluation. Jan's plan of action follows (column 8):

Column 8	PLAN OF ACTION

1. Increase individual therapy to once a week and use grief loss workbook as homework
2. Join eating disorders educational program so I won't use food to stuff down feelings
3. Write a good-bye letter to Grandma
4. Take letter and read it at Grandma's gravesite
5. Let go and affirm myself

PROBLEM-SOLVING METHODOLGY

Column 1	Column 2	Column 3	Column 4
ISSUES TO BE ADDRESSED	TARGET TOP ISSUE	OLD PATTERN OF BEHAVIOR	HOW DESTRUCTIVE TO ME
1.	1.	1.	1.
2.	2.	2.	2.
3.	3.	3.	3.
4.	4.	4.	4.
5.	5.	5.	5.

Column 5	Column 6	Column 7	Column 8
OLD MESSAGE	NEW MESSAGE	BRAINSTORMING	PLAN OF ACTION
1.	1.	1.	1.
2.	2.	2.	2.
3.	3.	3.	3.
4.	4.	4.	4.
5.	5.	5.	5.

The above process is widely used in many therapy settings. The concept is not unique, but it *is* an effective tool. Use the process to lead you out of the sleep in the Poppy Fields. You *must* take the time to work through the pain of the above steps or your sleep in the Poppy Fields may last forever!

WARNING: *Dorothy's return home was due to a change within herself. That change was the belief in herself. There is a difference between "making changes" and "change". Making changes are little steps resulting in a significant change. Change is the means of travel which leads us home.*

There's no place like home . . . There's no place like home . . .

6

No Place Like Home: The Integration of Dorothy

Dorothy closes her eyes and clicks her heels together quickly three times. She repeats over and over, "There's no place like home . . . no place like home . . . no place like home." Her mind whirls as she views the images of her past journey before her eyes: Auntie Em hanging clothes in the farmyard, Uncle Henry feeding the feisty pigs, Professor Marvel prophesizing her Aunt's sorrow, the Tin Man's creaky first movements, the Cowardly Lion's adorable smile, the Scarecrow's proud face when he got his diploma, and the Wicked Witch shriveling before the foursome. The images all wash together as Dorothy opens her eyes. She remembers what she had said only moments ago — "I won't look any further than my own backyard. Because if I do, it wasn't really there and I never really lost it to begin with!"

Together we have come to the end of our journey. Secretly we have given you a gift along the way. Our gift was within your grasp, just as it was within Dorothy's grasp.

Return to the beginning . . . go back to the first page and look once again at the bricks on the bottom of each page. Our brick road marked your pathway to this destination. To find our subliminal message you must fill in the following blanks with the letters at the bottom of every third page.

_ _ _ _ _ _ _   _ _ _ _   _ _   _ _ _ _ _ _ _
_ _ _ _ _ _ _ _ _ _ _ _ _ _ _   _ _ _ _ _ _ _
_ _ _ _ _ _ _ _ _ _ _ _ _ _ _

Now you have found Dorothy's secret! You never really lost it to begin with! All you had to do was look in *your own backyard!* Despite all the trauma, the pain, anger and loss, it was still inside — waiting for you to discover! You had to journey this far to truly value what you hold inside. Amazingly, you had saved your gift for yourself throughout it all. As you now realize, you always had the power within. It sounds so simplistic, but *you* are the *miracle* and can now feel safe dwelling with your "home".

Integration

Think back for a moment. Didn't the Lion show his courage in the castle courtyard before he got his medal? Didn't the Scarecrow have brilliant ideas all along? Wasn't the Tin Man's sensitivity apparent to us from the beginning?

We strive most of our lives to be recognized for our qualities, as if these qualities do not count unless we have the medal, the diploma or the outer heart to prove ourselves. These material items are nice to have, but they do not make us what we truly are inside.

Together they have taught you a precious lesson — you have what you desire inside and must take the risk and integrate it in your everyday life. Integrate that which you value within yourself and take the risk to try on the behaviors you desire to incorporate. This means that you must have the courage, the heart and the wisdom to trust yourself and give yourself what you have wanted from others — recognition of your strengths.

We have hopefully given you some down-to-earth hands-on methods to journey home. We have made you aware of the impending Poppy Fields and of the powers you possess. We have given you means to handle conflicts and have shared the journeys of others with you in the hope that this will make your journey a little easier and safer to begin.

Now you have one more important task. As you traveled through the "Progression and Recovery" sections of each of our main characters, we asked you to fill in your pictorial positives page with your positives from each role. Remember, you can have a combination of two or more roles, and it is important that you identify all of your positives. Don't sell yourself short. The following page is a pictorial version of Dorothy — use it to piece together your positives from the Scarecrow, the Tin Man, the Cowardly Lion, the Wizard and the Wicked Witch. Those parts that you desire for yourself should be added to this pictorial illustration. You can use characteristics from the role page, or issues from the treatment plans that you saw in the previous chapters, or other items to piece together each part of your puzzle.

Place within this drawing the positives that you possess from this role. Include with an asterisk (*) the characteristics you desire to integrate into your journey.

Collect all the positives and desired characteristics that you put inside the drawings of the Scarecrow, Tin Man, Cowardly Lion, the Wicked Witch and the Wizard of Oz. Place the information inside the outline of Dorothy. This is the integrated you. You had it within yourself all along! Take time to integrate what you desire. It's always been within your grasp.

There is one more word of warning — sometimes recovery is like the childhood game "Chutes and Ladders". We climb and struggle to get to the next height and sometimes, even with our best intentions, we slip down a bit when we aren't watching. You have the skills to nurture yourself at this time. Parent yourself with acceptance and love. Allow yourself patience, love and listen to your inner child. You must integrate your heart and your brain and have the courage to find what lives within! You will now know peace and serenity and will say "there's no place like home . . . no place like home . . ."

Recommended Reading

Ackerman, R. Children of Alcoholics: A Guide for Educators, Therapists and Parents, Holmes Beach: Learning Publications, 1983.

Bepko, C.; Krestan, J. The Responsibility Trap, New York: The Free Press, 1985.

Black, C. It Will Never Happen To Me, Denver: Medical Administration Co., 1981.

Black, C. Repeat After Me: A Workbook for Adult Children, Denver: Medical Administration Co., 1985.

Bloomfield, H. Making Peace with Your Parents, New York: Ballantine Books, 1983.

Carnes, P. The Sexual Addiction, Minneapolis: Comp-Care, 1983.

Cowan, C.; Kinder, M. Smart Women, Foolish Choices, New York: Signet Classics, 1985.

Deutsch, C. **Broken Bottles, Broken Dreams,** New York: Teachers College Press, 1982.

Fisher, B. **Rebuilding,** San Luis Obispo: Impact Publications, 1981.

Fossum, M.; Mason, M. **Facing Shame: Families in Recovery,** New York: W.W. Norton & Co., 1986.

Gorski, T.; Miller, M. **Counseling for Relapse Prevention,** Hazel Crest, IL: Alcoholism Systems Associates, 1979.

Gravitz, H.L.; Bowden, J.D. **Guide to Recovery: A Book for Adult Children of Alcoholics,** Holmes Beach: Learning Publications, 1985.

Halpern, H. **How to Break Your Addiction to a Person,** New York: Bantam Books, 1982.

Hope For Adult Children of Alcoholics, Minneapolis: Hazelden Lectures.

Kiley, D. **The Wendy Dilemma,** New York: Avon Books, 1984.

Kritsberg, W. **Adult Children of Alcoholics Syndrome: From Discovery to Recovery,** Pompano Beach: Health Communications, 1986.

Larsen, E. **Stage II Recovery,** Minneapolis: Winston Press, 1985.

Lerner, R. **Daily Affirmations for ACoAs,** Pompano Beach: Health Communications, 1985.

Maxwell, R. **Breakthrough: What to Do When Alcoholism or Chemical Dependency Hits Close to Home,** New York: Ballantine Books, 1986.

McConnell, P. **Adult Children of Alcoholics — A Workbook for Healing,** San Francisco: Harper & Row, 1986.

Milam, N.; Ketcham, K. **Under The Influence,** Seattle: Madrona Publications, 1981.

Norwood, R. **Women Who Love Too Much,** New York: Pocket Books, 1985.

O'Gorman, P.; Oliver-Diaz, P. **Breaking the Cycle of Addiction: For Adult Children of Alcoholics,** Pompano Beach: Health Communications, 1987.

Russionoff, P. **Why Do I Think I Am Nothing Without a Man?,** New York: Bantam Books, 1981.

Sexias, J.; Youcha, G. **Children of Alcoholics' Survivors' Manual,** New York: Harper & Row, 1985.

Subby, R. **Lost in the Shuffle: The Co-Dependent Reality,** Pompano Beach: Health Communications, 1987.

Typpo, M.; Hastings, J. **An Elephant in the Living Room,** Minneapolis: CompCare, 1984.

Wegscheider, S. **Another Chance — Hope and Health for the Alcoholic Family,** Palo Alto: Science and Behavior Books, 1981.

Wegscheider-Cruse, S. **Choicemaking,** Pompano Beach: Health Communications, 1985.

Whitfield, C. **Healing the Child Within,** Pompano Beach: Health Communications, 1987.

Wilson, A. **Co-Dependency,** Minneapolis: Winston Press, 1986.

Woititz, J. **Struggle for Intimacy**, Pompano Beach: Health Communications, 1985.

Woititz, J. **Adult Children of Alcoholics**, Pompano Beach: Health Communications, 1983.

Other Books By . . .

HEALTH COMMUNICATIONS, INC.

Enterprise Center
3201 Southwest 15th Street
Deerfield Beach, FL 33442
Phone: 800-851-9100

ADULT CHILDREN OF ALCOHOLICS
Janet Woititz
Over a year on The New York Times Best Seller list,this book is the primer
on Adult Children of Alcoholics.

ISBN 0-932194-15-X $6.95

STRUGGLE FOR INTIMACY
Janet Woititz
Another best seller, this book gives insightful advice on learning to love
more fully.

ISBN 0-932194-25-7 $6.95

DAILY AFFIRMATIONS: For Adult Children of Alcoholics
Rokelle Lerner
These positive affirmations for every day of the year paint a mental picture
of your life as you choose it to be.

ISBN 0-932194-27-3 $6.95

*CHOICEMAKING: For Co-dependents, Adult Children and Spirituality
Seekers* — Sharon Wegscheider-Cruse
This useful book defines the problems and solves them in a positive way.

ISBN 0-932194-26-5 $9.95

LEARNING TO LOVE YOURSELF: Finding Your Self-Worth
Sharon Wegscheider-Cruse
"Self-worth is a choice, not a birthright", says the author as she shows us
how we can choose positive self-esteem.

ISBN 0-932194-39-7 $7.95

LET GO AND GROW: Recovery for Adult Children
Robert Ackerman
An in-depth study of the different characteristics of adult children of
alcoholics with guidelines for recovery.

ISBN 0-932194-51-6 $8.95

LOST IN THE SHUFFLE: The Co-dependent Reality
Robert Subby
A look at the unreal rules the co-dependent lives by and the way out of the
dis-eased reality.

ISBN 0-932194-45-1 $8.95

Books from . . .
Health Communications

THIRTY-TWO ELEPHANT REMINDERS: A Book of Healthy Rules
Mary M. McKee
Concise advice by 32 wise elephants whose wit and good humor will also
be appearing in a 12-step calendar and greeting cards.
ISBN 0-932194-59-1 $3.95

BREAKING THE CYCLE OF ADDICTION: For Adult Children of Alcoholics
Patricia O'Gorman and Philip Oliver-Diaz
For parents who were raised in addicted families, this guide teaches you
about Breaking the Cycle of Addiction from *your* parents to your children.
Must reading for any parent.
ISBN 0-932194-37-0 $8.95

AFTER THE TEARS: Reclaiming The Personal Losses of Childhood
Jane Middelton-Moz and Lorie Dwinnel
Your lost childhood must be grieved in order for you to recapture your
self-worth and enjoyment of life. This book will show you how.
ISBN 0-932194-36-2 $7.95

ADULT CHILDREN OF ALCOHOLICS SYNDROME: From Discovery to Recovery
Wayne Kritsberg
Through the Family Integration System and foundations for healing the
wounds of an alcoholic-influenced childhood are laid in this important
book.
ISBN 0-932194-30-3 $7.95

OTHERWISE PERFECT: People and Their Problems with Weight
Mary S. Stuart and Lynnzy Orr
This book deals with all the varieties of eating disorders, from anorexia to
obesity, and how to cope sensibly and successfully.
ISBN 0-932194-57-5 $7.95

Orders must be prepaid by check, money order, MasterCard or Visa.
Purchase orders from agencies accepted (attach P.O. documentation)
or billing. Net 30 days.

Minimum shipping/handling — $1.25 for orders less than $25. For
orders over $25, add 5% of total for shipping and handling. Florida
residents add 5% sales tax.